BTRIPP BOOKS

BOOK REVIEWS FROM

2010

BY BRENDAN TRIPP

These reviews originally appeared on the
"BTRIPP'S BOOKS" book review blog:
http://btripp-books.livejournal.com/

Copyright © 2016 by Brendan Tripp

ISBN 978-1-57353-410-9

An Eschaton Book

Front cover photo courtesy Kenn W. Kiser via morguefile.com.
Back cover photo courtesy Sebastian Santana via morguefile.com.

PREFACE

From 1993 through 2004, I ran the *first* manifestation of Eschaton Books (now in its third revival). Initially started as a vehicle to publish my poetry, it soon became evident that the market for poetry is vanishingly small, and in 1994 we "pivoted" into being a metaphysical press.

In this time, I was largely a one-man shop, doing everything from editorial to shipping, which was a huge time commitment, and I typically worked 14 hour days, 7 days a week to keep things moving. I bring up all this here because, despite having been a life-long avid reader, during this period I had precious little time for reading, and what reading I *did* get done was largely reviewing book submissions. However, I never stopped *buying* books, which began to stack up in prodigious "to be read" piles.

When Eschaton went out of business in 2004 (in a not unusual denouement for a small press – we had a distributor who ended up never paying us, while selling through all our stock), I found myself with a lot of reading to catch up on, and a need to keep my writing chops sharp. So, I began to pen little reviews of what I was reading through, and post those on the web.

As the years went by, this became "a thing" that I was doing, and, for a while, I was targeting a fairly aggressive goal of getting at least 72 non-fiction books read per year. By 2015, this had resulted in my having read and reviewed 700 books over that 12-year span.

In recent years (since the upswing in print-on-demand publishing), I have had numerous acquaintances suggest that I put out my reviews as books. I was, at first, rather hesitant on the concept (as, after all, the material was free to read on the web), but I eventually figured that if various people thought it was a good idea, I might as well give it a shot.

While I could have started at the beginning, with the reviews from 2004, I decided that those were less representative of the whole, so opted to begin with the most recent ones.

This is the sixth of these collections, and is pretty close, with 71 reviews, in representing the 72+ books a year I was reading from 2006-2012. As noted in the Prefaces in previous volumes, the page count here is less than what it would be on later collections, as what I was targeting in terms of word-count on my reviews crept up over the past several years. So, this 2010 collection has four more reviews in it than the 2011 book, but ended up with exactly the same page count!

And, to repeat the note on my review "style": I do not write classic reviews, but more a telling of my personal interaction with a particular book. This means that I talk about where and how I got the book, how it relates to other things I've read, what sort of reactions it triggered in me (and why), and how one can get a copy if it sounds appealing. Needless to say, if the reader is devoted to "standard" book reviewing styles, this might be an irritation ... however, it does make these reviews somewhat idiosyncratic to me, resulting in a collection that is something of a "my encounters with books" sort of deal, which will, hopefully, be of interest to many readers.

- Brendan Tripp

CONTENTS

v - Preface

vii - Contents

1 - Friday, January 1, 2010

A good one ...
The Five-Minute Miracle
by Tara Springett

3 - Saturday, January 2, 2010

War, and stuff ...
Peace Kills: America's Fun New Imperialism
by P.J. O'Rourke

5 - Wednesday, January 13, 2010

Another near miss ...
Entangled Minds:
Extrasensory Experiences in a Quantum Reality
by Dean Radin

7 - Saturday, January 16, 2010

O.K. ...
How to Self-Destruct:
Making the Least of What's Left of Your Career
by Jason Seiden

9 - Wednesday, January 20, 2010

Not quite a tragedy ...
The Union of Their Dreams:
Power, Hope, and Struggle
in Cesar Chavez's Farm Worker Movement
by Miriam Pawel

11 - Sunday, January 24, 2010

If it's not about "Thriving", then ...
How to Thrive in Changing Times:
Simple Tools to Create True Health, Wealth, Peace,
and Joy for Yourself and the Earth
by Sandra Ingerman

13 - Monday, January 25, 2010

"The Goat"
A Chicago Tavern
A Goat, a Curse, and the American Dream
by Rick Kogan

15 - Sunday, January 31, 2010

You ... going from 1.0 to 2.0
Me 2.0:
Build a Powerful Brand to Achieve Career Success
by Dan Schawbel

18 - Saturday, February 6, 2010

I'm not that kind of Boomer, I guess ...
1001 Things It Means to Be a Boomer Now:
(Well, It Is Time to Grow Up)
by Harry H. Harrison Jr.

20 - Monday, February 8, 2010

Finally, one that makes sense ...
Crush It!
Why Now Is The Time To Cash In On Your Passion
by Gary Vaynerchuk

22 - Wednesday, February 17, 2010

It's super-freaky, Yow...
Super-Freakonomics:
Global Cooling, Patriotic Prostitutes,
and Why Suicide Bombers Should Buy Life Insurance
by Steven D. Levitt & Stephen J. Dubner

24 - Sunday, February 21, 2010

Nettle tea, anyone?
Songs of Milarepa
by Milarepa

26 - Sunday, February 21, 2010

Building Trust ...
Trust Agents:
Using the Web to Build Influence, Improve Reputation,
and Earn Trust
by Chris Brogan & Julien Smith

29 - Saturday, February 27, 2010

Doom and gloom ...
The Last Three Minutes
by Paul Davies

31 - Monday, March 1, 2010

Amazing ...
**CrazyBusy:
Overstretched, Overbooked, and About to Snap!
Strategies for Coping in a World Gone ADD**
by Edward M. Hallowell M.D.

33 - Sunday, March 14, 2010

So, you wanna be in pictures?
**Get Seen:
Online Video Secrets to Building Your Business**
by Steve Garfield

35 - Tuesday, March 16, 2010

It's Greek to me ...
In the Dark Places of Wisdom
by Peter Kingsley

38 - Monday, March 22, 2010

More at "encyclopedia" ...
**Social Media 101:
Tactics and Tips to Develop Your Business Online**
by Chris Brogan

40 - Sunday, March 28, 2010

Something "catchy" ...
**Viral Loop: From Facebook to Twitter,
How Today's Smartest Businesses Grow Themselves**
by Adam L. Penenberg

42 - Sunday, March 28, 2010

Not the end of the world?
**Fired!:
Tales of the Canned, Canceled, Downsized,
and Dismissed**
by Annabelle Gurwitch

44 - Saturday, April 3, 2010

Utopia ...
Utopia
by Sir Thomas More

46 - Sunday, April 11, 2010

A beautifully written book ...
The Writer's Voice
by A. Alvarez

49 - Sunday, April 11, 2010

Your mileage may vary ...
Ethical Ambition:
Living a Life of Meaning and Worth
by Derrick Bell

51 - Sunday, April 18, 2010

An essential for the job search ...
Use Your Head to Get Your Foot in the Door:
Job Secrets No One Else Will Tell You
by Harvey Mackay

53 - Monday, April 26, 2010

The earliest humans ...
Cro-Magnon:
How the Ice Age Gave Birth to
the First Modern Humans
by Brian Fagan

55 - Sunday, May 2, 2010

If you want to get technical about it ...
Social Media Metrics:
How to Measure and Optimize
your Marketing Investment
by Jim Sterne

57 - Sunday, May 2, 2010

And now for something completely different ...
On Guerrilla Warfare
by Mao Tse-tung

59 - Saturday, May 8, 2010

Like hiring a career counselor, only cheaper ...
Get The Job You Want Even When No One's Hiring
by Ford R. Myers

61 - Sunday, May 23, 2010

If only ...
**The 4-Hour Workweek:
Escape 9-5, Live Anywhere, and Join the New Rich**
by Timothy Ferriss

64 - Saturday, May 29, 2010

Good advice, no nagging
**10 Make-or-Break Career Moments:
Navigate, Negotiate, and Communicate for Success**
by Casey Hawley

66 - Sunday, May 30, 2010

Touring history ...
Traveler's Guide to The Ancient World – The Roman Empire: Rome and its Environs in the Year 300 CE
by Dr. Ray Laurence

Traveler's Guide to The Ancient World – Ancient Greece: Athens and its Environs in the Year 415 BCE
by Eric Chaline

Traveler's Guide to The Ancient World – Ancient Egypt: Thebes and the Nile Valley in the Year 1200 BCE
by Charlotte Booth

69 - Sunday, June 6, 2010

A beginner's manual for the business world ...
Effective Immediately: How to Fit In, Stand Out, and Move Up at Your First Real Job
by Emily Bennington & Skip Lineberg

71 - Thursday, June 10, 2010

Great info ... for corporate execs
**The Next Wave of Technologies:
Opportunities in Chaos**
by Phil Simon

73 - Friday, June 11, 2010

An oldie but goodie ...
Permission Marketing: Turning Strangers Into Friends And Friends Into Customers
by Seth Godin

75 - Tuesday, June 15, 2010

Dollar store dreams ...
Riding Toward Everywhere
by William T. Vollmann

77 - Sunday, June 20, 2010

I Tweet therefore I am ...
Twitterville: How Businesses Can Thrive in the New Global Neighborhoods
by Shel Israel

79 - Monday, June 28, 2010

Retro reading ...
The Magic of Thinking Big
by David J. Schwartz

81 - Monday, July 5, 2010

Science!
Collider: The Search for the World's Smallest Particles
by Paul Halpern

84 - Friday, July 16, 2010

Digging it ...
The Maya
by Michael D. Coe

86 - Saturday, July 17, 2010

I only wish it worked that way ...
KaChing: How to Run an Online Business that Pays and Pays
by Joel Comm

88 - Sunday, July 18, 2010

If you can ...
Cash In A Flash: Fast Money in Slow Times
by Mark Victor Hansen & Robert G. Allen

90 - Saturday, July 24, 2010

In my kids' world ...
Rewired: Understanding the iGeneration and the Way They Learn
by Larry D. Rosen, Ph.D

92 - Sunday, July 25, 2010

This we could use!
Careers For Your Cat
by Ann Dziemianowicz & Ann Boyajian

94 - Saturday, July 31, 2010

When gestures have meaning ...
What Your Body Says (And How to Master the Message): Inspire, Influence, Build Trust, and Create Lasting Business Relationships
by Sharon Sayler

96 - Sunday, August 1, 2010

I'd love to go there ...
Angkor: Temples of Cambodia's Kings
by Dawn F. Rooney

98 - Friday, August 6, 2010

Stealth fundie spew ...
What Bothers Me Most about Christianity: Honest Reflections from an Open-Minded Christ Follower
by Ed Gungor

101 - Saturday, August 7, 2010

Yes, a non-boring book on business ...
Rework
by Jason Fried, David Heinemeier Hansson & Mike Rohde

103 - Sunday, August 8, 2010

Difficult to read, but thought-provoking ...
Glenn Beck's Common Sense: The Case Against an Out-of-Control Government, Inspired by Thomas Paine
by Glenn Beck

106 - Friday, August 13, 2010

More than meets the eye ...
On Seeing: Things Seen, Unseen, and Obscene
by F. Gonzalez-Crussi

108 - Monday, August 16, 2010

No, not like THAT ...
The Art of Business Seduction: A 30-Day Plan to Get Noticed, Get Promoted, and Get Ahead
by Mark Jeffries

110 - Saturday, August 21, 2010

OOOPS ...
Mutant Message Down Under
by Marlo Morgan

112 - Sunday, August 22, 2010

If you can define your goal ...
Well Connected: An Unconventional Approach to Building Genuine, Effective Business Relationships
by Gordon S. Curtis

115 - Monday, August 30, 2010

How to be "remarkable" ...
Free Prize Inside: How to Make a Purple Cow
by Seth Godin

118 - Tuesday, August 31, 2010

CAUTION: new age spewage ahead ...
The Secret of Shambhala: In Search of the Eleventh Insight
by James Redfield

120 - Tuesday, September 7, 2010

Paranoid ...
Whispers: the Voices of Paranoia
by Ronald K. Siegel

122 - Wednesday, September 8, 2010

Bad, bad Bubba ...
No One Left To Lie To: The Triangulations of William Jefferson Clinton
by Christopher Hitchens

124 - Sunday, September 12, 2010

Too many cooks ...
The Twitter Job Search Guide: Find a Job and Advance Your Career in Just 15 Minutes
by Susan Britton Whitcomb, Chandlee Bryan, & Deb Dib

126 - Saturday, September 18, 2010

English lit ...
Snake and Other Poems
by D.H. Lawrence

128 - Sunday, September 19, 2010

Notes on the Universe ...
The Grand Design
by Stephen Hawking & Leonard Mlodinow

131 - Monday, September 20, 2010

This is how you do it ...
UnMarketing: Stop Marketing. Start Engaging.
by Scott Stratten

133 - Tuesday, September 21, 2010

A perfect match ...
Vitamin Q: A Temple of Trivia Lists and Curious Words
by Roddy Lumsden

135 - Sunday, October 3, 2010

Social media for social change ...
The Dragonfly Effect: Quick, Effective, and Powerful Ways To Use Social Media to Drive Social Change
by Jennifer Aaker, Andy Smith & Carlye Adler

137 - Sunday, October 17, 2010

But not really ...
A World Without Islam
by Graham E. Fuller

140 - Tuesday, October 19, 2010

A useful little book ...
**The Illustrated Timeline of Religion:
A Crash Course in Words & Pictures**
by Laura S. Smith

142 - Monday, October 25, 2010

Like a cat needs a self-help book ...
**Who Moved My Mouse?: A Self-Help Book for Cats
(Who Don't Need Any Help)**
by Dena Harris & Ann Boyajian

144 - Friday, October 29, 2010

Not that strange ...
Strange Maine: True Tales from the Pine Tree State
by Michelle Souliere

146 - Monday, November 1, 2010

Don't judge this book by its cover ...
**The New Job Security, Revised: The 5 Best Strategies
for Taking Control of Your Career**
by Pam Lassiter

148 - Saturday, November 6, 2010

Isn't that convenient ...
**The Secrets of Judas: The Story of the
Misunderstood Disciple and His Lost Gospel**
by James M. Robinson

150 - Saturday, November 13, 2010

The Heart of America ...
**The Mom & Pop Store:
True Stories from the Heart of America**
by Robert Spector

152 - Sunday, November 21, 2010

Write ... right ...
**Be a Brilliant Business Writer: Write Well, Write Fast,
and Whip the Competition**
by Jane Curry & Diana Young

154 - Saturday, November 27, 2010
A really remarkable book ...
Tribes: We Need You To Lead Us
by Seth Godin

157 - **QR Code Links**

177 - **Contents - Alphabetical By Author**

183 - **Contents - Alphabetical By Title**

Friday, January 1, 2010[1]

A good one ...

As I've noted in this space before, I'm a participant in the LibraryThing[2] "Early Reviewers" program, which from time-to-time provides me with books (matched to my on-line collection via the mysterious workings of "The Algorithm") to read and review. I have been fortunate to have received books in each of the past 3 months (with copies-to-requests odds of 5.9%, 3.4%, and 2.3%), with this being one of the better books that I've had from that source.

I initially was a bit hesitant about The Five-Minute Miracle[3] by Tara Springett, as it had numerous "newage" red-flags in my view, but I was fascinated, as I got into reading it, to find that it potentially (disclosure: I've not attempted *practicing* the system described as yet) is grounded on more substantial stuff that many books that it may resemble! The "5 minute miracle" of the title is the 2-minute, twice a day visualization practice that Ms. Springett has named "Higher Consciousness Healing". As frequent readers of my scribblings may recall, I have studied Vajrayana Buddhism, which Ms. Springett is also rooted in. A substantial factor in Vajrayana is visualization practices which often take the form of a particular symbol (be it a Tibetan syllable, or an object) in a particular color, focusing on which is designed to produce a particular effect. In essence, this is what the author's "Higher Power Healing" is based upon.

However, the author is also a psychotherapist, and this discipline comes in during the preparatory phases. The first part of the process here is to identify what needs to be addressed. One has to do a bit of work to narrow down the range of the "problem" and what one is specifically feeling regarding that. She postulates three basic types of feelings that are causing one's suffering, *anger*, *sadness*, or *anxiety*, (with a table to relate these to a wider range of emotions) and that these manifest in various ways in various situations. Also, she has one focus on the problem in terms of the emotions it produces, i.e., one does not suffer from *being* fat, one suffers from feelings of frustration about not being able to lose weight. She also has one *rate* how much one generally suffers from the problem, from a 0 (no suffering) to a 10 ("utter desperation").

Once one has the problem defined in these terms, it's time to contact one's Higher Consciousness for assistance. She uses a consciousness model which involves the day-to-day Conscious mind, the Unconscious mind, and the Higher Consciousness, which she defines in something of a pan-theistic mode of a greater level of consciousness which is shared by all beings. Despite being shared, each person is likely to envision their Higher Consciousness in a particular form, from a religious symbol, to some newagey manifestation. Through a process of relaxation exercises (basic self-hypnosis) one gets to a point where one encounters one's Higher Consciousness, and gets, through this, images of one's "Life Path", which provides a general "map" of how one is presently progressing. Once one has this information, one is to ask one's Higher Consciousness for a "symbol" to help one overcome one's suffering specific to the previously-defined problem. Interestingly, if one does not *like* the symbol one initially gets, one is encouraged to ask for a different one!

Once one has one's symbol, one goes through a fairly simple meditative practice to focus on it, for two minutes, twice a day, for a minimum of two weeks. She suggests "adding" this to some pre-existing habitual action (like brushing one's teeth), so that it will be easier to have on-going. At the end of two weeks, one takes assessment of how one is suffering (that 0-10 scale) and adjust one's activities appropriately. Interestingly, Springett claims that nearly all of her clients have *substantial* improvement in the initial two weeks, some achieving complete relief of the specific suffering in that period.

Again, I have not attempted to do this practice myself as yet, so I can't give much *direct* feedback on that, but the component parts, the visualization, the self-hypnosis, the mediation, all are dead on things that I *have* experienced, and the combination here looks like it would have every chance of working. The author claims that the method "popped up" in her mind, perhaps after a long period of mulling around various elements in her subconscious, in search of "a method of transpersonal psychotherapy" to help with her own issues. I, personally, would have liked the book more had it grounded its assorted aspects in the background practices (that I, at least, perceived to be behind it), but it does seem to have solid theoretical basis, and could be a very useful approach. As The Five-Minute Miracle[4] is just now coming out, you're best bet is likely getting it on-line (Amazon has it at 28% off of cover), but if you're looking for something in this ballpark, this is a fascinating practice that has a lot to recommend it!

Notes:

1. http://btripp-books.livejournal.com/86464.html
2. http://btripp-books.com/
3-4. http://amzn.to/1VRbt3Z

Saturday, January 2, 2010[1]

War, and stuff ...

This was one of those "dollar store finds" that I was amazed to see in that context. After all, P.J. O'Rourke is a major author, and is still with the same publisher, and this book is relatively recent (2004, with the paperback out in 2005), so why in the dollar store? The only thing I could think was that they dumped the hardcover, go figure.

Anyway, P.J. O'Rourke's Peace Kills: America's Fun New Imperialism[2] was a nice find for a buck. It's a collection of pieces initially published in *The Atlantic Monthly* between 1999 and 2003. Obviously, "article collection" books are probably the simplest things to get into print, as all the "heavy lifting" of researching, writing, and editing are *already done*, and there is frequently a considerably variability in the final product, depending on how well the pieces were selected, how well they work in conjunction with each other, and how they stand as "a book" as opposed to one which had been written to be a single entity. The over-all theme of this is more "America & War" than the *fun new imperialism* of the sub-title, and O'Rourke has, conveniently, written from many war zones over the years. However, each of these pieces is self-contained for a particular conflict, event, or occurrence, and there is very little holding the whole together.

Now, I was quite enthusiastic as I plowed into this, eagerly spinning through the first half or so, but at some point it just began to drag, and I found myself somewhat *relieved* to finish it. This is not to say that the component articles aren't informative and entertaining in their own right, it's just that at some stage, there seemed to cease to *be a point*, and began to read something like a Nexis article return from a search on "war" and "O'Rourke". Perhaps if this had sat in a "bathroom reading" stack and been read in drips and drabs over a period of weeks or months, it would have stayed "fresher" than having been the "currently reading" feature in my recent schedule. Again, there aren't really any "clunkers" in here, it's that that the whole is perhaps less than the sum of its parts.

As far as subject matter is concerned, the book starts with "Kosovo – November 1999", which focuses on the "down the rabbit hole" aspects of the UN/Clinton adventure in the Balkans; it then moves to "Israel – April 2001", with a look at the bizarre "permanent conflict" in the middle east, and how mundane and relatively bloodless (he quotes fatality figures merely *in the hundreds* and compares them to "civil wars you never heard of" which killed tens of thousands, if not millions) this has been; next up is "9/11 Diary" which are his notes of the odd state of Washington DC following the attacks there and in New York, and the strange responses arising around the country (oh, and re-written lyrics to "The Banana Boat Song" which are hilarious); his next stop is "Egypt – December 2001", which is more of a cultural/historical piece than anything really related to either the USA or warfare, except for the constant complaint that "Osama has ruined the tourist business"; next come "Nobel Sentiments" where he examines one of the evergreen idiocies coming from the Nobel Prize crew (I wonder how he covered B.O.'s recent prize for the remarkable feat of *not being GWB!*), proving that being a "Nobel Laureate" does not necessarily mean that one is not a moron; at this point he moves on to *another* batch of morons in "Washington DC Demonstrations – April 2002" where a "Palestinian Solidarity March" had turned into something fairly basic (some Palestinian-American groups staging a march) into a zoo of the lunatic left (with dozens of specific examples of the extent of such lunacy); after a brief interlude, "Thoughts on the Eve of War", O'Rourke takes us back to the middle east with "Kuwait and Iraq – March and April 2003" which largely focused on the civility and rationality of the Kuwaitis and the feral mob aspects of the Iraqis, both in the looting and the lack of even basic cultural ethics; finally, there is "Postscript: Iwo Jima and the End of Modern Warfare – July 2003" where he goes (as part of a team working on a documentary) to the tiny, yet iconic, battle site from WW2, and reflects on the history and nature of war.

Again, as noted above, this is all "good stuff", and (piece by piece) is quite entertaining and informative, but it probably should be consumed in those bite-size bits over a period of time rather than at one intense push. This is still available in the paperback, so should be available via your local brick-and-mortar book vendor, but "very good" copies of the hardcover are available from the new/used guys for a penny, with "new" copies coming in just over a buck, so if you can't find this at *your* local dollar store, those are options for getting it. Peace Kills[3] may not be O'Rourke's finest moment, but it is a collection of thoughtful impressions of some very interesting conflicts, and may well be something that would fit in your library.

Notes:

1. http://btripp-books.livejournal.com/86686.html

2-3. http://amzn.to/1SNQ2jB

Wednesday, January 13, 2010[1]

Another near miss ...

I'd ordered Dean Radin's Entangled Minds: Extrasensory Experiences in a Quantum Reality[2] due to its association with Lynne McTaggart's *The Intention Experiment*. Those of your who read my review[3] of that may recall that I was mainly enthusiastic about the various scientific studies reported there. I had hoped that this book was going to be more of same, and, I suppose, it *is*, but in a far more muted form.

Frankly, this is less a book *about* Psi phenomena than it is some *apologia* "calling out in the wilderness" regarding how Psi has been unfairly stigmatized, mocked, and ignored. The author looks for support in history, noting how many famous people, noted organizations, etc., had held psychic/spiritual phenomenon to be proven fact, and then tip-toes into the experimental area. Unlike McTaggart, who covered really "mind blowing" results in her book, Radin seems to concentrate only on the most iron-clad variable-controlled tests, frequently ones only looking for the most subtle and non-dramatic results, and then putting the aggregated data from large collections of these to the most rigorous statistical analysis. For the average reader, this produces a response of "oh, that's *nice*", and something of a yawn for those "in the choir" as it were. It's as though Radin wrote the book *for skeptics* only to have it marketed to the *enthusiast* audience!

This is not to say that he doesn't eventually dip a toe into what would be "radical" areas, it's just that by the time he's set up the ground work, he's likely lost the core readers. In the latter half of the book he does touch on these:

> (in presentiment experiments) what you find is a spectacular body of converging evidence indicating that our understanding of time is seriously incomplete. These studies mean that some aspect of our minds can perceive the future. Not infer the future, or anticipate the future, or figure out the future. But actually perceive it.

... covering the idea that our concept of time, and space/time, is likely in need of further consideration, how various government projects (both in the US and Russia) have had rather dramatic results (now largely available via FOI Act requests), and what might be possible with some more dedicated research ... but it still reads like he's talking about the *deli* and not the *sandwich*, focusing on the slicer and not the flavor.

Does this make Entangled Minds[4] a *bad* book? No ... there is certainly a lot of interesting stuff in here, especially in the minutia of how you do statistical analysis on these sorts of studies, but I guess when I ordered this (and I actually paid Amazon's discounted *retail* for it!) I was hoping for the "WOW!" factor that is clearly present in the various more challenging studies in the field, and I didn't come away with much of that. Rather than having a book-length tour of the stuff that McTaggert leads off with in her book, this was more like a behind-the-scenes look at how these studies get legitimized.

Again, there is a feel throughout that he's *pleading* for the skeptics (and the off-hand dismissers) to take a look at the (considerable) evidence for there "being something real" about Psi phenomena, and, perhaps, this is the best use of the book ... as an introduction to the subject to those hard cases who habitually reject all things psychic.

This is, of course, in print, and the new/used guys don't have it at much of a break (Amazon currently has it at 28% off of cover), so if you're interested in picking up copy you might as well go the retail route. It isn't, however, the "wow!" book you might guess it to be from its title. Oh, and, you can do a *wicked* re-write of Elvis' "Suspicious Minds" riffing off of the title ("*... we can talk through the ether, with Entangled Minds; and have prophetic dreams, with Entangled Minds ...*") if you're so inclined!

Notes:

1. http://btripp-books.livejournal.com/86892.html
2. http://amzn.to/1poxKlk
3. http://btripp-books.livejournal.com/79284.html
4. http://amzn.to/1poxKlk

Saturday, January 16, 2010[1]

O.K. ...

For somebody who, until just recently, *never* read any "business" books, I find myself in an odd situation of being on the receiving end of numerous offers to get review copies of various job search and career management titles, due, no doubt, to my recent penning of The Job Stalker[2] blog on the Chicago Tribune's "Chicago Now" blogging site, and my more recent inclusion of book reviews and author interviews there. The current book, Jason Seiden's How to Self-Destruct: Making the Least of What's Left of Your Career[3] came to me through an unusually convoluted route, not being something that I bought, or got from Library Thing's "Early Reviewer" program, or even had come from the *author* (@seiden on Twitter), but came from *another* Twitter user, Melissa Cooley of The Job Quest[4] blog (@TheJobQuest) who had obtained a number of his books and was doing a give-away of them on *her* blog.

Needless to say, How to Self-Destruct[5] is *not* your average career-management book. Nominally targeted to those who would want to have the least amount of career success, it speaks to the voice of counter-intention within us all, and (one supposes) uses this in a "reverse psychology" subterfuge to shake up the reader on a rather reflexive level. The book has 14 main chapters broken into four general sections: *Taking Down Your Career, Kicking Your Career When It's Down, Laying Waste to Your Personal Environment*, and *Mastering the Self-Destruction Process*. Each chapter is in two parts, the main part, and pages with a red tint called "Surefire Masochistic Alternatives" for whatever style of "success seeker" is the flip side of the main chapter's focus (i.e., "for Rookie Success Seekers" in the "Falling Down On You First Job" chapter).

Frankly, I felt the book worked best in the first half, as the chapters pretty much follow along a typical career path there, and the back-and-forth between "nightmare advice" and the far more hard-nosed suggestions in the "masochistic alternatives" are in very clear parallel ... almost like a career-guide version of the old Goofus & Gallant[6] morality plays in *Highlights for Children*. The second half of the book is more general "lifestyle", uh, *advice*, and gets a bit hazier in its good/bad mirroring, and thereby feels less effective than the parts which are essentially showing Goofus doing the wrong things for a successful career, then showing hard-working, considerate Gallant doing all the right things. Also, both sides of the "lifestyle" equation come across as a bit "naggy", lacking the "case by case" presentation of the work scenarios, and having a very "judgmental" feel (oddly in *both* the approaches) which serves to just make the reading uncomfortable, as opposed to ironic or instructive.

While, obviously, the book should be asked to stand or fall on its own merits, it is helped by a wander through Seiden's web site[7] which repeatedly asks the reader to *"dare to fail spectacularly"*. Within the context of Seiden's *other* material, the "fade away" of How to Self-Destruct[8] is less dramatic, as the book sort of blends towards other things that Seiden "is on about", but it would certainly be a far stronger work had it maintained the mirroring of the early chapters. His site is, however, a rather rich source of similar material, so if the book speaks to you (my wife snagged this while I was reading it and was a good deal more enthusiastic about it than I have been), there's a lot more to dig into there.

This is currently in print, so you should be able to get it at your local brick-and-mortar book vendor, but Amazon has it at a discount, and if you combine it with some other stuff to get up to the free-shipping promised land, you'll do better than even going with the used guys. Again, this is a "whole different approach" to a career book, and it could certainly be seen to be pushing past the bounds of "ironic" into the realm of "sarcastic", but if you're in the mood for something along those lines (some time spent on Seiden's site should give you a "feel" for this), do go get yourself a copy.

Notes:

1. http://btripp-books.livejournal.com/87069.html
2. http://www.chicagonow.com/blogs/job-stalker/
3. http://amzn.to/1qRDHOq
4. http://rodneysjobquest.wordpress.com/
5. http://amzn.to/1qRDHOq
6. http://blogs.chicagotribune.com/news_columnists_ezorn/2006/06/goofus_gallantt.html
7. http://jasonseiden.com/
8. http://amzn.to/1qRDHOq

Wednesday, January 20, 2010[1]

Not quite a tragedy ...

As readers of my main blog are certainly aware, I've been penning one of the Chicago Tribune's "Chicago Now" blogs, The Job Stalker[2] (detailing the course of my own job search) for the past several months. Out of contacts made through that, I was recently invited to be a participant in the "Signature Club", a feature of the Trib's Book Section's Printers Row[3] blog that brings in "reader reviews" from the public. This was how I came to be reading Miriam Pawel's The Union of Their Dreams: Power, Hope, and Struggle in Cesar Chavez's Farm Worker Movement[4] (which had been, oddly enough, also a feature of the LibraryThing.com "Early Reviewer" program).

I must admit, The Union of Their Dreams[5] was *not* something that I would have been likely to have picked up in "free range" book shopping, but I'd suggested that I'd probably do a better job reviewing a *non-fiction* book, and this was what the Trib sent. I was relieved to find that this book was largely a *historical* approach to the United Farm Workers rather than a *doctrinal* screed.

As I worked my way through the book, I developed quite an admiration for the research that author Miriam Pawel had done to produce this document. As opposed to being an *external* view of the United Farm Workers, with information collected from news stories, etc., or a "personal" view, this was an *internal* look at the *"la causa"* through the stories of various participants. Notably absent from this list is Cesar Chavez, while being *the* pivotal figure for the ultimate story arc, this is a look at the lives and involvement of numerous key players, from Mexican lettuce cutters and irrigators who moved from the fields to be top union figures to "idealistic" White kids looking for some "meaningful experience", like one who is described as:

> Ellen was looking for a meaningful experience before heading to graduate school in social work. She knew nothing about the lettuce boycott and wasn't too sure of the difference between Cesar Chavez and Che Guevara. But the internship sounded in line with her career goals, and she was eager to see California.

The book is broken into six "themed" blocks of time which present different phases of activity, from the initial grape strike in 1965 to Chavez's death in 1989, each further divided into chapters on specific events and issues. What makes the book stand out is that, within these chapters, the narrative follows various players' activities in those contexts. That the author was able to dig up enough source information to make these individual sections read plausibly as part of a historical overview is quite impressive, and that at no point does the tone waver from the over-all flow of the book is quite a testament to Ms. Pawel's writing skill.

While clearly being the story *of* Cesar Chavez's movement, the book is a story *about* a dozen or so individuals. There is Chris Hartmire, a young "activist" minister; Elisio Medina, a grape harvester who joined the union as a teen; Jerry Cohen, a navy brat turned counter-culture lawyer; Sabino Lopez, a second-generation irrigator in the lettuce fields; Ellen Eggers, the social work student in the above quote; Sandy Nathan, a draft-dodging anti-war protester turned lawyer; Gretchen Laue, a kid who was looking for temp work and ended up with the boycott office in Boston; and Mario Bustamante, a top-ranked lettuce-cutter from Mexico City (as well as several other "recurring characters" who did not get their own sections). The story moves from vignette to vignette of these people's experiences, and in the process weaves the general tale of the union.

It is *not* a pretty story, nor, ultimately, particularly flattering of Mr. Chavez. All of the key players end up "purged" eventually. Chavez, while claiming "loyalty" as a prime virtue, showed little of it himself, as long-time close friends are shed in alternating cynical and paranoid organizational shake-outs. Chavez envisioned himself as some sort of near-messianic figure, reading about Gandhi, but associating with the likes of Philippine dictator Ferdinand Marcos and Synanon cult leader Chuck Dederich (aspects of which Chavez attempted to install as a "new religion" within his "movement"). The core "tragic" element in the book is that gulf between what was, initially, an extremely effective "roots" labor movement which truly revolutionized the state of the farm worker and what Chavez envisioned as his grander "poor people's movement". Somehow the latter always managed to trump the former, and any disagreement with Chavez was framed as "treason", so time after time, contracts were left unfinished, programs not actualized, even checks uncashed due to random re-allocations of staffing resources.

If you have an interest in labor, agricultural, or political issues, this book should appeal to you. It also provides an interesting window on a certain area of counter-cultural activities from the sixties, seventies, and into the eighties. As The Union of Their Dreams[6] is new, your local brick-and-mortar book vendor should have it, although Amazon has it at 34% off and there are already copies at deeper discounts in the new/used market. Again, this is not something that I would have been likely to read "on my own", but it certainly rewarded my attention with a fascinating tale of a notable time in our history.

Notes:

1. http://btripp-books.livejournal.com/87458.html
2. http://www.chicagonow.com/blogs/job-stalker/
3. http://featuresblogs.chicagotribune.com/printers-row/
4-6. http://amzn.to/1XVOEto

Sunday, January 24, 2010[1]

If it's not about "Thriving", then ...

Sometimes books that I really *want* to like just don't connect with me, and I find the reading somewhat uncomfortable. This is a prime example of this scenario. I got Sandra Ingerman's How to Thrive in Changing Times: Simple Tools to Create True Health, Wealth, Peace, and Joy for Yourself and the Earth[2] via LibraryThing.com's "Early Reviewer" program last month (the third month in a row that I'd "won" a book there), so there was that slight disconnect anyway (in that I hadn't really reached out to *acquire* it, only indicating that I'd be willing to review it), but the book wasn't really what I was expecting.

Ms. Ingerman is, apparently, a "newage shaman" and does workshops and is involved in assorted "trade associations" along those lines. This book has the "feel" of something that would accompany a workshop program, but really addressing "soccer moms" or the like, as it relies very little on the reader having *any* background in esoteric subjects. Now, as long-term readers of this space will recall, I've both been studying various forms of Shamanism for over a quarter century, and have very little patience for "fluffy bunny light working". The combination of these two factors probably "sets me up" for having a difficult time attempting to productively interface with this book.

Now, this "thriving" concept is something that I've seen cropping up more and more in various contexts, and I'm not sure if it's a legitimate cultural meme or simply the "concept *du jour*" among the newage crowd. Unfortunately, there's not much specifically about "thriving" (at least on a personal basis, the author keeps coming back to a concept she calls the "healing the earth quotient", which might be where she envisions this happening) in the book, but a lot of "small exercises" that are sort of "shamanism lite" which would, admittedly, serve as a functional toe-dip into the mystical for the cliché bored suburban housewife. As I kept reading, I kept getting more irritated, wanting her to "get to the point", only to realize that there was NO point she was "getting to" here, only a process, an introduction, and something of a guidebook for somebody who'd attended a weekend workshop (or something of the sort) to continue on with on their own.

It also seemed to me that Ms. Ingerman spends a lot more time than most authors I've read promoting her organizations, friends, and websites in the book. I can't say if she's doing this as "presenting her credentials" or simply flogging a marketing opportunity, but it's something that stood out to me as being "above and beyond" even the newage norm. And, speaking of "newage norms", the book has a lot of that "if we just think bright shiny thoughts the whole world will be new and nice and there won't be anything bad in it anymore" vibe to it, and I was bumping up against that with some good solid cynicism over and over again.

Given the above, you might well think that I ended up *hating* the book, and this is (oddly enough) *not* the case. Frankly, there are several substantial bits of information, from the existential (avoiding negative inputs like the news, avoiding presenting oneself in ways that will generate negative social vibes, etc.) to the esoteric (looking at the dynamics of "group action"), to the practical (a *fabulous* exercise to develop a *visceral* sense of "attraction" using strong magnets). Some of the stuff in here is a bit on the fringe (I was wondering if she'd attempted any double-blind experiments on some of the physical things she claims to have been able to effect), and a *lot* of it is off in the fluff-bunny zone, but there are enough "solid bits" that reading the book was at least worth the time I invested in it.

Again, I was probably looking for one thing in the book, and the author was presenting another. I would have *much* preferred this if it was about *Thriving* on a conceptual and/or philosophical basis, bringing in concrete examples as needed to illustrate and bolster the main material. Instead this is a workbook which feels like it's targeted to folks with little or no mystical/occult background, framed in "Green" contexts to make it palatable. If one *is* in this "target audience" then How to Thrive in Changing Times[3] might well be a great introductory book to start doing work of this kind, but if one is simply looking for insight into, well, *how to thrive in changing times*, you might find yourself as disconnected from it as I was.

Obviously, as an "Early Reviewer" book, this has just come out (it even has a 2010 copyright date), so is likely to be at your local brick-and-mortar book store, although Amazon has it for less than ten bucks (reasonably priced for having less than 200 pages). This really wasn't "my cup of tea" but it did have enough solid material in it that it wasn't a waste of time ... obviously, I'm a bit of an "outlier" on the "esoteric reading" scale, so (in the immortal jest of Dennis Miller) *"your mileage may vary"*, and I suspect that *most* folks wouldn't have the same points of irritation that I was finding with various aspects of the book!

Notes:

1 http://btripp-books.livejournal.com/87612.html

2-3. http://amzn.to/1qRC9UH

Monday, January 25, 2010[1]

"The Goat"

The other evening, in my never-ending search for "networking" events that might eventually lead to my *finding a job*, I attended a TweetUp hosted by @ColonelTribune[2] in honor of the launching of the new "TribNation" venture under the aegis of @JamesJanega[3]. While the scope of the "TribNation" concept is still a bit hazy to me (it seems to involve one-on-one contact with readers via assorted Social Media vehicles), the Trib certainly had an eye on history and continuity in opting to have the bash at Chicago's fabled *Billy Goat Tavern*, a long-time watering hole and refuge for the "ink stained wretches" of the Tribune (and other papers, most now gone).

The party, which ended up being quite a smash, involved having us wearing jaunty newspaper hats (as has been recently modeled by the Colonel himself in his Twitter icon), and circulating between groups of folks, some from the paper, some from Twitter, and some from the extended blogosphere (I ran into folks that I'd known from assorted other networking events, other Chicago Now bloggers who just popped into The Goat for a *cheezborger*, and got to meet various editors, managers, and columnists, such as the noted writer of the Ask Amy feature). To top off the festivities, "door prizes" of Rick Kogan's A Chicago Tavern: A Goat, a Curse, and the American Dream[4] were awarded, my getting one (I take it) for having been the first to arrive.

A Chicago Tavern[5] is one of those books that feels almost accidental, as though the writer (who I discovered is a product of the same Chicago high school that I graduated from) had started to do a feature story about The Billy Goat and found the subject getting away from him, as its length (115 pages with about 25 of those being extremely charming photographs) does not suggest a *"I'm going to write a book about The Goat!"* genesis. As one would expect from this, it is a quick, but quite entertaining, read. The book weaves various histories together, the stories of the Sianis family, immigrating in waves from Greece, first William (Billy), then his nephew Sam (who still presides at the saloon, and was around for the party), and their various relatives; the story of the newspaper business in Chicago, and how The Goat was a favorite of not only the writers, but the pressmen and other laborers from the half-dozen or so newspapers that used to publish within blocks of the bar; and the story of the mass-media attention, of the old *Saturday Night Live* crew, and how the *homage* to the Billy Goat was no cynical ploy, but rooted in John Belushi's Albanian immigrant relatives who also operated "Greek diners" when he was growing up.

However, as the sub-title indicates, this is ultimately a story of the much-tarnished American Dream, centered on the Sianis family, and what Billy and Sam were able to build over the better part of a century after coming here with *nothing* (Billy arrived with $5.00 which was scammed off of him even before he got out of Ellis Island, only to be recouped many years later, as detailed in a remarkable reminiscence). All sorts of fascinating bits and pieces come out here. Sam Sianis was interested in "getting the real story out" and worked extensively with Kogan to get the information right. For instance, the whole "goat" angle came about by happenstance, but Bill Sianis saw the possibilities and re-shaped his own image to the "billy goat" iconography, and how the whole "Cubs Curse" was invented to help sell papers long after the initial snub of Billy and his goat (although it would appear that the Wrigleys were extremely opposed to allowing a goat into the stands, whether or not it had a ticket). Also touching is the tale of how newspaperman Mike Royko and saloonkeeper Sam Sianis came to be extremely close friends, "better than a brother", and much of the decor in the bar is memorabilia of the late Chicago scribe.

Needless to say, I greatly enjoyed A Chicago Tavern[6] and would highly recommend it to all and sundry, and especially those with an interest in Chicago history, newspaper lore, immigrant stories, and cultural memories. As a "small book" its cover price is fairly low, and Amazon has it as a discount, but those of you who are either in Chicago or are planning on coming here can also get a copy (along with some awesome *cheezborgers*) at the Billy Goat!

Notes:

1. http://btripp-books.livejournal.com/87989.html
2. http://twitter.com/coloneltribune
3. http://twitter.com/JamesJanega
4-6. http://amzn.to/2414LNm

Sunday, January 31, 2010[1]

You ... going from 1.0 to 2.0

Well, this is the first time that I've *really* felt that I needed to make obsequience to the invasive scrutiny of our vile governmental masters, but in the interest of staying on the right side of the FTC's ridiculous regulations I figured I should note that the copy that I have of this book came from the publisher at the request of the author in order that I would have a copy to read and review. As regular readers are no doubt aware, I've been getting review copies from other sources (LibraryThing.com's Early Reviewer program, the Chicago Tribune, etc.) for quite some time, but this is the first instance of my being directly contacted by an author for the purpose of having me do a review. Obviously, we have *always* been at war with Eastasia. Needless to say, my recent tenure as the writer of The Job Stalker[2] blog on the Trib's "Chicago Now" site, and my now-regular review/interview feature for books about the job search and related subjects, has begun to draw some attention to my long-obscure scribblings (I have been doing these reviews in this space for several years at this point), and we wouldn't want to have the FTC *fine me* for receiving a free copy of a book, would we?

Anyway, the book which has led me across this particular Rubicon is Dan Schawbel's Me 2.0: Build a Powerful Brand to Achieve Career Success[3], a book about Schawbel's *own* "brand" of personal branding. In retrospect, it's no surprise that I had "some issues" with this book, as it is *explicitly* targeted to "Generation Y" or "Millennials" (which I was *shocked* to find includes my grade-school-aged daughters!), and pretty much only deals with aging Boomers like myself in a sense that we should go ahead and *die* to make room for the new, hipper, generations. As I was *only* reading this as a part of my OWN job search, I found this both irritating and unsettling, as, within the context of the book, people my age are pretty much regarded as obstacles to be tossed aside in the path of the favored groups' career advancement!

Fortunately, most of that stuff is contained in Part 1 of the book ("The Rise of Personal Branding"), which is focused fairly firmly on the Gen Y audience (with 30 years of professional experience, the "extracurricular activities" of *my* college days rarely come to mind, let alone find a way into my "personal brand"). The "meat" of the book commences with Part 2 ("Command Your Career In Four Steps"), which presents some *very* useful (even for geezers like myself) materials for creating what Schawbel describes as one's "brand", divided in sections "Discover Your Brand", "Create Your Brand", "Communicate Your Brand", and "Maintain Your Brand". Again, for somebody who has been "organically" developing (however unconsciously) a "brand" for a few decades, some of the steps involved in here are either in the *"been there, done that"* category, or *"that horse is already out of the barn"* zone, but over-all the materials presented in this part of the book are very well thought out, "systematic" (in the sense that a network marketing program is a "system"), and reasonably applicable to anybody at the point of focusing on their career (it did cross my mind that my 14-year-old daughter could benefit from reading this).

While much of the initial material is *extremely* basic (what's appropriate business dress, etc.), it certainly seems to be *comprehensive*, walking the reader through such foundational skills as business writing, verbal presentation, confidence building, constructive persistence, developing technical competence, how to make a sales pitch, etc. Again, the examples given here are generally that of 20-year-olds with minimal work experience, trying to differentiate themselves in the entry-level (or not, he adds in examples of *numerous* folks who had reached upper-level jobs by 24) job market. The same level of detail is exhibited as the book moves to web sites, blogs, and social networks, giving step-by-step instructions on how to conceptualize, execute, develop, and market these vehicles, with (and here's the part I found most useful, personally) fairly extensive notations of on-line and other resources for doing this.

The tone of the book is somewhat uneven, vacillating between specific instructional segments, and Schawbel pontificating on his *own* (admittedly, rather remarkable – he's only four years out of college at this point) experience. On this latter point (if you'll excuse a jaded late-Boomer bit of attitude), he *does* point out that this sort of success only comes with *"the right combination of skill, determination, networking, and timing"*, to which I might add *luck* in being in the right place at the right time with a message specifically in resonance with the *Zeitgeist*. Needless to say, Schawbel is an "outlier" who achieved remarkable success in an amazingly short period of time (and he details several others who have been similarly unusually successful).

This brings me to my main criticism of the book ... while it does have a "system" that should be applicable in its general outlines to anybody reading it, it is very likely *not* going to result in finding oneself in "C-level" positions by age 24 unless one has extremely high levels of both skill (and the ability to "pick up" things with little very little study and practice) and determination. On this latter point, in a section on "tenacity", Schawbel says: *"(entrepreneurs) get very little sleep because they realize the opportunity cost in sleeping instead of getting things done"*. While I certainly *agree* with this statement (and for decades have lived *my* life according to that pattern), I'd submit that the percentage of the population that is willing to *drive* themselves to the extent that the book suggests is vanishingly small. So, going in, one has to realize that if you don't have the ability to pick up skills quickly and effectively, and if you're fond of watching TV, hanging out with friends, or having much of any "free time", you're probably *not* going to create the sorts of success on which the book focuses.

Again, this is not to say that there isn't a whole lot of useful information and advice in here (indeed, there were many "new tricks" this "old dog" is likely to be taking from reading it), only one needs to keep in mind what one is bringing to the table. Much like most network marketing pitches, this is long on what *could* happen, while avoiding much consideration of what an "average result" would be. The "personal branding" meme may have actual application in the evolving work force, but for *most* people, jumping though the hoops of developing one's "brand" is only likely to have subtle benefits (confidence, focus, etc.) and not land one in the executive suite, with media stardom, or on lucrative lecture tours.

Me 2.0[4] should be available at your local brick-and-mortar book vendor, although Amazon has it for about 1/3rd off. This is certainly a "your mileage may vary" sort of a book, if you're a Gen Y kid looking to break big in the business world, this might just be your "user manual", but for Boomers looking to maximize what's left of their careers, maybe "not so much".

Notes:

1. http://btripp-books.livejournal.com/88138.html
2. http://bit.ly/4JYua5
3-4. http://amzn.to/1VR6QHe

Saturday, February 6, 2010[1]

I'm not that kind of Boomer, I guess ...

I have something of an annual ritual now, thanks to being on Barnes & Noble's mailing list. The past several years, they have had a *significant* clearance sale after the holiday clearance, the post-holiday clearance, and the post-post-holiday clearance, where in the stores a couple of big tables of books are just $2, and on the web site there are sections for $1.99, $3.99 and $5.99 clearance books. On the web site there were nearly *800* clearance books for $1.99 ... and I set about finding enough (13 – mostly hardcovers) to get over $25.00 and score free shipping (which was a good thing as the shipping on the order would have been about seventeen bucks!). Obviously, in this shopping mode, there were things selected because they "sounded interesting" rather than being things I had a burning desire to read ... this is one of those.

I only knew the broad strokes about Harry H. Harrison Jr.'s 1001 Things It Means to Be a Boomer Now: (Well, It Is Time to Grow Up)[2] when I added it to the cart, but after reading a few things rather "Gen Y"-oriented, I felt like delving into something "my generation", the ancient, aging Boomers. Frankly I had expected something more of a "joke book" ... and being in the desperate career impasse that I have been for the past year or so, I was *looking forward* to something that was heavier on the humor. Unfortunately, this is more a collection of wry, bordering on cynical, jabs at the Baby Boom generation, focused more on the clichés than on what has been *my* generational experience, making this a bit more of a stressful read than I had anticipated.

The book is, as one would expect from the title, a collection of 1001 observations on Boomers, generally directed *to* boomers with the tone that might typically accompany *"you have some spinach stuck in your teeth"* or *"you've got something all over the back of your coat"*. These are divided into thematic sections: Generation Gap, Getting Physical, Forever Young, Working For The Man, Financial Security, Surviving The Sexual Revolution, Husbands And Wives, Home Is Where The McMansion Is, Growing Up, Single Boomers, Technical Details, Our Children Ourselves, Your Parents Sill Don't Understand You, Rock And Roll Never Died, Boom Times, Everything Is Spiritual, Boomer Men, Boomer Women, Boomers In Midlife Crisis, Boomer Grandparents, You And Your Pets Are One, and How Boomers Think. Generally speaking, the author seems to have a mental image of the Boomer being an ex-hippie, Rolex-wearing, technologically-challenged, over-paid professional who lives in the suburbs in a house substantially beyond his/her means, is on their third marriage, and has only a very tenuous grasp on reality. While the last point may be applicable, I found it hard to relate to any of the rest, despite being a boomer.

Attempting to summarize this beyond the descriptions above seems somewhat pointless, so instead, I guess I'll just pick out a few things that seem illustrative:

> 22. Being a Boomer means you think wrinkles are optional.
>
> 55. Being a Boomer means having a boss young enough to date your son.
>
> 131. Being a Boomer means refusing to give up your weight training even though you have to take Vicodin for your back.
>
> 207. Being a Boomer means deciding that if a doctor isn't going to give you a pill for your pain, you'll change doctors.
>
> 241. Being a Boomer means having some people mistake you for your child's grandfather.
>
> 287. Being a Boomer means wondering not about a second career, but a third or a fourth.
>
> 394. Being a Boomer means considering a part-time job at Starbucks because of the benefits. And the deals on espresso shots.
>
> 427. Being a Boomer means you find your wife sexier than you did thirty years ago.
>
> 548. Being a Boomer means thinking a flash drive has something to do with Star Trek.
>
> 634. Being a Boomer means learning the ins and outs of Medicare.
>
> 671. Being a Boomer means you have a wine collection that's worth the cost of a car.
>
> 736. Being a Boomer means understanding that maybe, just maybe, it isn't all about you.
>
> 907. Being a Boomer means giving your dog only Evian to drink.
>
> 986. Being a Boomer means you're still searching for meaning.

Needless to say, "your mileage may vary" on how this stuff reads ... I found the book, while wry, generally depressing, but that's likely due to my own personal situation. Also, it turns out this is from a "preachy publisher" so there's a lot of more of "the G word" (and I don't mean *gangsta*) in here than one would anticipate from a mundane press. 1001 Things[3] appears to still be "in print", as it is only a couple of years old (despite going out via clearance at B&N), and Amazon has it for 42% off of cover, and their new/used guys have "like new" copies for as little as a penny, so if this sounds like a laugh-fest to you, you're likely to be able to find a copy.

Notes:
1. http://btripp-books.livejournal.com/88489.html
2-3. http://amzn.to/1VR5NXD

Monday, February 8, 2010[1]

Finally, one that makes sense ...

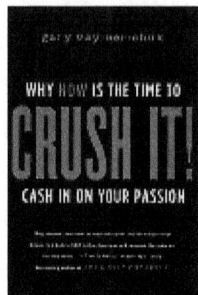

As those of you paying attention here may have noted, I've started going through a lot of "business" books, much against my historical reading patterns. Obviously, most of these have been in the "job search" or "career management" vein, relating to my own in-search-of-employment endeavors, reinforced recently by my penning the Chicago Tribune's "Chicago Now" blog, The Job Stalker[2], which has both caused me to buy books suitable for coverage there, and recently to be offered review copies.

Gary Vaynerchuk's Crush It! Why Now Is The Time To Cash In On Your Passion[3] is one of the books that I *bought*, having seen it referenced so frequently in other books and on Twitter, that I figured that I really needed to add this to my reading list. I've been focusing a good deal of my recent attention of Social Media, as, frankly, there is a lot more call for it in the current Web than Virtual Worlds.

I am *very* glad that I picked up Crush It![4], as it "spoke to me" in a way that many of the other books in the "future of work" or "personal branding" niches haven't. Perhaps it is Vaynerchuk's style, he's talking about how he did what he did, why he did what the did, and how he saw what he did in context of the wider economic landscape, in a very "conversational" mode (indeed, he mentions that he pretty much just *talked* about this into a recorder, and then sent it off to a writer to pull together into a book). As opposed to a book like Finding Work in the 21st Century[5], which pontificates on the "new world" of no jobs, but independent contractors, this shows what that could look like, *not as some dystopian future* but as a current exciting, engaging, and rewarding career path *today*. As opposed to a book like Me 2.0[6] this is also not an attempt to set up a "system" for the most driven young professionals to reach the early and gaudy success, but a look at how *one* (equally driven) guy made this work with the tools and resources he had in his life. Having read the other two books certainly made me appreciate this more, as (while firmly in that world-view) it's a very real and vivid illustration of not only how this can work, but how it can be a great adventure rather than an oppressive grind. While utilizing most of the *specifics* that Schawbel preaches in *Me 2.0*, Vaynerchuk isn't advocating an obsessive drive to super-successes, being very clear on what steps would be necessary to replace an average drag-into-the-office-everyday salary with income from activities linked to what one knows well, and what is one's passion. Also, this is more "ethically based" than most, with the author constantly framing activities within the context of how actions effect those around us.

Where the other books mentioned above might be a white paper on how the work world as we've known it is doomed, and a "manual" for devising a personally-branded career, this gets far more into the "why" while still detailing the "what" and "how". While the style is easy to read, the book is quite *dense* with material (probably a good thing, as it is only a slim hundred and fifty pages!), neglecting step-by-step instructions for descriptions of broad-stroke processes and lists of needed activities. A reminder, however: this is a book for the "driven", which is fine for an obsessive-compulsive fellow like me, but a lot of the world is not wired that way ... here's a bit of a caveat Vaynerchuk presents:

> *You will do (those steps) over and over and over again as long as your brand exists. If that sounds tedious or repetitive, just close this book and go do your best to enjoy the life you've got because you're not cut out for this.*

... I can't help but wonder what the "future" is for the folks who just punch the clock for a paycheck and spend the rest of their lives in search of distraction.

My regular readers are no doubt tired of my habit of rolling through chapter headings to give a sense of the book, but this is one of those books where it is a useful approach. I'm going to highlight and paraphrase to an extent here, however: "Passion is Everything" ... "Build Your Personal Brand" ... "Create Great Content" ... "Choose Your Platform" ... "Create Community" ... "Make The World Listen" ... "Start Monetizing" ... "Legacy Is Greater Than Currency" (oddly, this list is pretty much *every other* chapter). The main message here is to identify your passion, play to your strengths (he talks about the difference between text, audio, and video), and staying true to your vision.

Again, if you have an interest in Social Media, and "Web 3.0", you *really* need to pick up a copy of Crush It[7] ... it has to be "essential reading" for the evolution of the new economy. Needless to say, you should be able to find copies of this anywhere, I got mine through Amazon who had it at about 1/3rd off of cover (and, interestingly, the used guys don't have copies for much less than that). *Highly* recommended!

Notes:

1. http://btripp-books.livejournal.com/88717.html
2. http://bit.ly/4JYua5
3-4. http://amzn.to/1qRt26i
5. http://btripp-books.livejournal.com/85828.html
6. http://btripp-books.livejournal.com/88138.html
7. http://amzn.to/1qRt26i

Wednesday, February 17, 2010[1]

It's super-freaky, Yow...

Oh, yeah, tell me *you* don't hear Rick James' funk classic when the title of this book comes up! I don't know exactly what prompted me to order Levitt & Dubner's Super-Freakonomics: Global Cooling, Patriotic Prostitutes, and Why Suicide Bombers Should Buy Life Insurance[2], except that I'd read its predecessor, *Freakonomics*[3] a few months back. As is often the case in the movie biz, the sequel seemed (to me, at least) much weaker than the original.

The subjects here, while "fascinating" in their own rights, I suppose, were (generally speaking) more diffuse and less pointed than those of the first book. The first chapter, nominally about prostitution, started out strongly enough (especially for a Chicagoan) in dealing with the Everleigh Club, and wandered into comparisons of top-end escorts vs. street whores, then looked at pimps in relation to *Realtors*, and eventually got into the career options for modern women, which somehow led to the conclusion that one of the challenges the country has been having is that top-notch women, who in generations past would have been likely to have ended up as stellar school teachers, are now ending up with MBAs and pursuing a wide range of other options, leaving the teaching jobs to, well (as the old saw would have it) "those who *can't*". Again, this drifts around quite a bit, and one keeps wondering where the actual focus is. The second chapter, supposedly on terrorists, also begins oddly looking at sports and birth dates and family relations, before moving into terrorism (with the observation that, like many "name" revolutionaries, most terrorists come from the mid-to-upper class, and that one can *"think of terrorism as civic passion on steroids"*), and veering into the aftermath of 9/11 and from there into a look at Craig Feied's efforts with emergency medicine and computer systems, which then led back into a look at how to use computers to profile the likely terrorists in any given population! The third chapter looks at "apathy and altruism", and is largely anchored by the Kitty Genovese story (the "apathy factor" of which appears to have been greatly exaggerated by the press at the time), moves into a look at various social situations (like every time the ACLU wins some "prison rights" case, the crime in the involved state tends to spike), and a wide array of psychological experiments dealing with these factors. The fourth chapter is on "cheap and simple", and goes from Ignatz Semmelweis (the guy who first got doctors washing their hands to prevent infection) to various economies of food, and fuel, and into vaccines and how governments are usually the worst agents (due to "the law of unintended consequences") to enact effective change, this then tails into the question of seat belts (and studies that were done which showed that seat belts are at least as effective as protecting kids as car seats), and eventually into talking about Nathan Myhrvold and his system for simply and cheaply controlling hurricanes.

This sets up the "best" chapter in the book, both in terms of "gee whiz!" factors, and in terms of getting people's panties in a knot. Chapter 5 deals with "climate change" and how over-blown, exaggerated, politicized and sensationalized it has been. I'm surprised the Vegans haven't picked up the book as their new rallying point, as the authors very clearly show that cows, pigs, sheep, goats, etc. have *far* more effect on the climate than factories, trucks, and SUV's, and that (by extension) the whole thrust of the current "global warming" alarmism is *economic*, aimed at harming 1st world societies, and not actually addressing the problem (such as it is), which leads into a look at what economists call "externalities". This also comes back to Nathan Myhrvold and his partners in Intellectual Ventures (including Bill Gates, with projects like the laser mosquito killing device just recently featured at a TED conference[4]), and some of the (again) cheap and simple solutions that *they* have come up with to easily control climate issues. Needless to say, the true believers in the ~~scam~~ Church Of Climate Change (whose favorite "nightmare scenarios" the book quotes the I.V. guys saying *"don't have any basis in physical reality in any reasonable time frame ... no climate model shows them happening"*) are as apoplectic over this as various interest groups were on things in the first book!

Again, SuperFreakonomics[5] is both informative and entertaining, but is really not up to the punch of its predecessor, drifting and meandering from data point to data point, losing a lot of "oomph" on the way. Of course, it is well worth having, if for nothing other than watching Al Gore fans bust blood vessels over the "heresies" involved in showing that their crusade is largely a scam! It's only been out a few months, so is no doubt available via your local brick-and-mortal book vendor, although Amazon has it for a *whopping* 42% discount (which, in the book biz foodchain, is almost the price the wholesaler *buys* books from the distributor), which is pretty hard to pass up. While I found this weaker than *Freakonomics*, it's certainly a good read, and I'm happy to have it both in my head and in my library!

Notes:

1. http://btripp-books.livejournal.com/89019.html
2. http://amzn.to/1lmclm0
3. http://btripp-books.livejournal.com/84471.html
4. http://www.physorg.com/news185463943.html
5. http://amzn.to/1lmclm0

Sunday, February 21, 2010[1]

Nettle tea, anyone?

As regular readers of this space no doubt will tell you, I am a big fan of ordering my books through Amazon ... while I realize this is unpopular in some circles (I certainly appreciate the experience of brick-and-mortar book stores, but on-line ordering is how I get most of my reading). One of the attractions of buying through Amazon (and B&N) is the reasonably low $25 threshold for free shipping, and one of the "sports" involved in this is seeing just how close to $25 one can get ... which is where Dover Thrift Editions come in so handy!

I picked up Songs of Milarepa[2] (no author/translator is noted, aside from "H.C." in the preface) in order to make a $23-something order into a $25-something order, being a perfect example of how one of these books can both save me some money, and add to my education. Now, as long-time readers know, I've read, studied, and experienced (I've taken five Vajrayana initiations) a good deal of Tibetan Buddhism, so came to this book as a "filling in the gaps". While I was certainly *familiar* with Milarepa, I could not recall specifically delving into his writings, except in context of the teachings in general.

This is where I first encountered some difficulties here (and was interested in finding out who had done the translation and occasional commentary) ... I've read a lot of Tibetan material (in translation, of course), and am used to a certain "tone". Now, this book is a republication of a 1958 book, and the direct knowledge of Tibetan culture was somewhat rare at that time (not non-existent, but hardly what it's been in the past decades), so there may be a reason for this not "sounding right" ... in fact, the preface here starts out trying to make Milarepa "the St. Francis of Tibet", saying *"there is the same lyricism, the same tender sympathy, the same earthiness, ... all nature was friend as well as chapbook"*, which (to my recall) is to try to push the Buddhist imagery of Milarepa into a wholly ill-fitting box, as his actual *teachings* are of non-attachment and the transitory nature of this existence!

Milarepa (his name comes from his personal name Mila, and "Repa", an honorific for "cotton clad", or a yogi who has mastered the *Tummo* exercises of "inner heat" and is thereby able to survive in snowy mountains with just a cotton robe) was a youth who had achieved a certain notoriety as a "black magician" before seeing the error of his ways, and becoming a student of Marpa, in the lineage of Naropa. Marpa was a very demanding task master, and Milarepa fled his yoke, only to return after some time with another teacher. Eventually Milarepa became the classic image of the hermit monk, subsisting on nettles in a high-mountain cave, although he did have students, including Gampopa who went on to found the Kagyu school.

Not knowing who *translated* this collection, I can't really speak to "where they were coming from", but it seems to me that this was done by a person who, while competent to read Tibetan, really didn't have an appreciation for the religion, and so was constantly trying to make Milarepa a "St. Francis". Frankly, there are parts here which almost sound like "boast" lyrics, which seems totally contrary to the spiritual focus of non-attachment, and all through the focus is often on the acts of individuals, rather than the inter-relations of levels of being and manifestation.

One very useful thing here, however, is the 15-point glossary in the back of the book, which gives concise thumbnails of assorted "doctrine points" from Tibetan Buddhism, from the classic "triple refuge" to the "ten virtues" and "the six doctrines of Naropa" ... a very handy "cheat sheet" to have if one is reading through Tibetan texts!

Obviously, had this book cost a lot, these concerns would make it less than attractive, however, the *cover price* of Songs of Milarepa[3] is a paltry $2.00 ... and at that, one can appreciate it for what it is, and gladly take its Glossary in the bargain. Again, this is an *ideal* book to "keep in reserve" for when you need to nudge up an order into that "over $25" free-shipping promised land. I assume that this (being still in print, and all) would be *available* from your local brick-and-mortar book vendor, but I doubt they'd be particularly enthusiastic about special ordering it in at that price point!

Notes:

1. http://btripp-books.livejournal.com/89197.html

2-3. http://amzn.to/1rgglCC

Sunday, February 21, 2010[1]

Building Trust ...

Maybe I've been "drinking the Kool-Aid" too much, or maybe it's just because (in my own job search) the areas of Social Media, "personal branding", and their various quasi-PR cognates ("web content", "reputation management" and all) seem to be where the opportunities are opening up. Whatever it is (and certainly regular readers of this space will have noted the trend), the genres of "job search" reading and "social media" reading have begun to significantly blur together in my mind.

As you probably know, I've been penning the Chicago Tribune's "Chicago Now" blogging site's The Job Stalker[2] blog for the past few months, and have brought in reviews from my LiveJournal accounts into there, paired with brief author interviews, for a feature that I've been trying to run on a weekly basis. Initially I was "re-using content" with reviews that I'd previously written here, then I had a few appropriate books come in via the LibraryThing[3] "early reviewers" program, then I had a couple of authors (or friends of authors) contact me, but this is the first time that I've actually queried a publisher to obtain a book ... so, for the benefit of the FTC: I was sent a free copy of this book by its publisher so that I would be able to read it in order to write a review. So don't fine me, OK?

Anyway, in the Twitter-centric world in which I've been living over the past year, Trust Agents: Using the Web to Build Influence, Improve Reputation, and Earn Trust[4] by Chris Brogan and Julien Smith is a fairly "big deal", with Brogan's blog ranked #3 on the AdAge "Power150". It has been fascinating to follow Chris' activities around the book, from anticipating its release last fall, through the seemingly non-stop travel that he does to promote it. However, as I was specifically interested in Trust Agents as "content" for The Job Stalker it did occur to me, when I sat down to write this review, that for *most people* this is not a "job-search book" ... or at least they're not likely to *realize* that it is at this point. As those of you who have been following along at home as I looked at books by McGowan[5], Seiden[6], Schawbel[7], Vaynerchuk[8], et al. I'm beginning to see that the "personal brand" may well be the core element of the Job of the future, so these may be more on target than they seem at first glance.

Of the books I've read in this niche, Trust Agents[9] is, perhaps, the most *philosophical* ... not a particular call to action, not a "manual", nor some dire warning of cultural change, this offers up a lot of the background rationale why one should re-invent oneself for these new realities. This is not to say the book isn't *instructive*, flipping through the various bookmarks I'd stuck in, I found that nearly all were for "action points" (from suggestions for setting up a web "listening station" to various services, systems, and programs one might consider using for achieving assorted tasks) rather than quotes.

There was one bit that I did want to pass along (largely for my *The Job Stalker* audience), where the "job" issue is addressed:

> *Being a trust agent requires a mix of strategies and skills that also serve other careers well. Thus, if you want to view what you've learned from this book in a different way, consider applying your new knowledge to your career at large. ... Though this book was written as a business book about using the web, the skills of a trust agent can be applied to many endeavors. If you think about it, this is another chance to make your own game. Perhaps you'll learn how to adapt your trust agent skills to other roles offline and have similar success.*

So, just what *is* a "trust agent"? At one point they describe it like Malcolm Gladwel's "connectors" (of the "connectors", "mavens" and "salespersons" of [The Tipping Point](#)[10]), people who seem to know everybody, far exceeding the sorts of limits implied by Robin Dunbar (where humans seem to have a capacity of maintaining "authentic relationships" with only about 150 persons – the "Dunbar number"). The book walks through various elements of becoming this, from *Make Your Own Game*, in which you're encouraged to re-define how or what you do; *One Of Us*, on how to become an authentic part of a community; *The Archimedes Effect*, how to leverage your skills, connections, and existing structures (like the web); *Agent Zero*, how to establish and support a network; *Human Artist*, developing the people skills that will give you the advantage; to *Build an Army*, obtaining leadership skills to make your efforts expand well beyond your own actions. Again, this is not a "how to" book as much as it is a "why do" book, with guidance, but not dictates, provided.

One thing I found very interesting here is that it was *very* good at anticipating my questions ... there were two or three points when I was thinking "but what about *this*", only to turn the page to find that "this" being addressed! I read a whole lot of books, and this is the first time I can recall noting this sort of "finger on the pulse" of a book's readers. I'd also like to share a story about Chris ... as I've noted, I've been following him on Twitter for quite a while, and he's written a lot about the genesis and expansion of the book. One thing that I'd never heard an author do (and, remember, I *ran* a publishing house for ten years) is that when he's "cooling his heels" in an airport terminal, he'll offer the various book vendors to sign all the copies they have of the book ... which is a *brilliant* gesture, benefiting the book, the retailer, and the customer, with nearly no effort on his part ... *that's* applying "leverage".

Needless to say, I very much enjoyed reading [Trust Agents](#)[11] and thank Wiley for sending me a copy. In situations where I've gotten a free book, I feel a bit churlish talking about the pricing, but this is available widely, from your local book monger to Amazon and B&N ... and those are likely your best options at the moment (Amazon has it at 34% off of cover), as the book is still popular enough that the "used" guys don't have it at much more of a discount that the retail channels. If you're interested in how to be more integrated into the new "trust economy", this is definitely something you should consider reading.

Notes:

1. http://btripp-books.livejournal.com/89349.html
2. http://bit.ly/4JYua5
3. http://btripp-books.com/
4. http://amzn.to/1oPcs6H
5. http://btripp-books.livejournal.com/85828.html
6. http://btripp-books.livejournal.com/87069.html
7. http://btripp-books.livejournal.com/88138.html
8. http://btripp-books.livejournal.com/88717.html
9. http://amzn.to/1oPcs6H
10. http://btripp-books.livejournal.com/77024.html
11. http://amzn.to/1oPcs6H

Saturday, February 27, 2010[1]

Doom and gloom ...

I don't know if I've mentioned it in the context of a review as yet, but once again this winter I took advantage of the after-after-holiday sale at Barnes & Noble, and got in a slug of books. I have, in the past, done this at the local store (where I happen to be writing this), but this year the sale came to my attention via the computer, so I sallied forth to the B&N web page to see what could be found ... of the $1.99 special books. I ended up getting 13 assorted titles, which (of course) put my order into that delightful free shipping zone, which was a good thing because the shipping would have been pushing twenty bucks on the order! Why do I detail this? Well (aside from adding some color and personal narrative, of course), there is a significant difference between books I bought *because they were $1.99* and books I've ordered because I was interested in obtaining *that particular book*. Obviously, I'm not likely to order (even at under two bucks) a book in which I have *no* interest in reading, but frequently these books are not the most *compelling* (to me, at least) reads. On the plus side, it does lead me to pick up titles which are somewhat "outside the box" from my typical studies.

The current book, Paul Davies' The Last Three Minutes[2] is not particularly in this category, as I have another *ten* books by him in my library[3] ... but it is something that I would likely have not gone in specific search of. The title is a play on Steven Weinberg's book *The First Three Minutes* (which deals with the Big Bang and the very early development of the universe), this being a look at *the end of the universe*, although only a couple of scenarios have anywhere near the focus of a given three minute period!

As regular readers of this space know, I read a fair amount of "popular" (as opposed to academic) books on physics. One of my issues with Davies is that he frequently seems to be over-simplifying his coverage of subjects, providing a (this is purely my bias speaking, I suspect) a *grade school* version as opposed to an "non technical" college-level rendition of the subject. Being that Prof. Davies *is* a university instructor, perhaps he knows better what will succeed in getting through to people in general, but I have read much in the general subject area, and nearly all of that was based on far more detailed analysis.

One notable thing here, however, is his focus on how *humanity* will be effected by these various doomsday events. Given that nearly all of the occurrences play out over many *billions* of years, most sensible people would sort of shrug their shoulders and say "what are the odds of us making it that long?". However, Davies (I just discovered) is a Templeton Prize recipient, which puts much of his orientation into that "with a grain of salt" zone, as this prize is given (in Richard Dawkins' phraseology) *"usually to a scientist who is prepared to say something nice about religion"* ... which would also go a long way to explain the tone of his *Are We Alone?*, which puzzled (and irritated) me at the time I was reading it!

Anyway, the book primarily deals with the "big two" universal death scenarios, endlessly expanding into a cold, empty void, thinly spread with the burned-out ashes of stars, galaxies, and possibly evaporating black holes, or reaching an ultimate expanse at which point gravity begins to win at everything starts coalescing back towards a fiery conflagration and an eventual massive singularity. There are also assorted *other* theories mentioned, including one that I'd not really encountered previously which asks something along the line of "what if this isn't the stasis state" and that assorted key parameters of the universe were simply in temporary states that might suddenly "tunnel through" to a more stable configuration which would involve phase shifting into states where, for instance, matter as we know it couldn't exist. Ooops.

Again, his focus is very much on how our descendants might deal with these various existential threats, which seems to be to be almost *bizarrely* anthropomorphic. There have been substantially better discussions of this in other books which posit "some galactic civilization" of some sort that had been around for billions of years attempting to address these challenges. Here one gets the sense that Davies is imagining Biblically-created human beings and not some functionally unimaginable product of environmental (or bio-engineering ... although he *does* address that possibility) evolution over remarkably vast stretches of time.

A U.S. paperback edition of The Last Three Minutes[4] is still in print (the copy I got from B&N was, oddly enough, a U.K. paperback), so you could perhaps find this at your local brick-and-mortar book vendor, but I'd recommend going through Amazon's new/used guys, who have "very good" copies for as little as two cents (plus shipping). Unless you were looking for a *very* "introductory" introduction to these concepts, you could do better book-wise, so why spend the money on the "Templeton-tainted" watered-down version?

Notes:

1. http://btripp-books.livejournal.com/89640.html
2. http://amzn.to/1VAQUbG
3. http://btripp-books.com/
4. http://amzn.to/1VAQUbG

Monday, March 1, 2010[1]

Amazing ...

This was one of those dollar store finds that really surprised me ... I picked it up because the title <u>CrazyBusy: Overstretched, Overbooked, and About to Snap! Strategies for Coping in a World Gone ADD</u>[2] pretty much describes my life in my seemingly never-ending job search. By Edward M. Hallowell M.D., an expert in Attention Deficit Disorder, the book was only vaguely the way I'd supposed it was going to be, and instead presented a "diagnosis" in the first half and a "treatment" in the second.

I had expected more of a "preachy" book about the bad habits that I and the rest of "type A" society exhibits, but the book deals more with humor and wry assessments than nagging, taking on, for example, the illusion of connection with TV shows: *"(Today Show viewers) get the warm feeling that comes from connection the same way trompe l'oeil imparts the feeling of three dimensions. Close inspection, however, reveals that it's a trick."* The author also has a whole vocabulary of made-up words to describe issues in the modern world, such as *Gemmelsmerch* for "the ubiquitous force that distracts us from what we're doing", and things such as "F-state" where one is frantic, frenzied, forgetful, flummoxed, frustrated, fragmented, etc. (as opposed to the "C-state" which is calm, cool, collected, etc.). Other words he introduces are *Screensucking*, time spent interfacing with TVs, computers, cell phones, and the like; *Leeches & Lilies*, the former being people and projects that suck your time and energy, while the latter are those which leave you fulfilled and satisfied; *Doomdarts*, which are obligations you've forgotten about that suddenly pop up and create panic; *Gigaguilt*, the feeling of the difference between what one *can* keep track of and what one *expects* oneself to keep track of; *Taildogging*, excesses indulged in out of the fear that not doing so will leave one behind the pack; *Frazzing*, inefficient multi-tasking; and many others.

Dr. Hallowell frequently compares the modern "F-state" with ADD, where the brain becomes a souped-up racing car, but *"The chief problem with this race car brain is that its brakes do not work well ... it can win races if it develops adequate brakes, but it will crash and burn if it doesn't."* About halfway through the book he congratulates the reader for having made it that far, suggesting that many will simply "eat" the book in random chunks, and not actually *read* it! Interestingly, he picks out the popularization of air conditioning as the one technology that began the "speeding up" of the culture, and the diverging into small individual boxes, interfacing with more technology than people.

The second part of the book is called "creating a system that works for you" defined this way:

> The central solution I offer in this book is this: <u>Make sure you do what matters most to you.</u> Everything else in this

> book is offered in support of that one goal. In order to reach it, you must regain the measure of control you ought to have and live actively, consciously, according to a system *you* have formulated yourself, which includes the creation of a positive emotional environment and your life's right rhythm.

To this end he provides various exercises, charts, and suggestions. One is very close to the 24/7 timesheets that I developed for my job search, which enable me to both make sure I'm putting in "enough hours" looking for work, but that I'm also not falling below a certain threshold for sleep. He has a three-factor "scoring system" which lets one determine what is valuable to you, which assigns an "effort" score between 1 and 5, a "fulfillment" score between 1 and 5, and a further "necessity" score between 1 and 5. An activity can rank between 1 and 125, with a 1 requiring maximum effort, being least fulfilling, and not being necessary, while a 125 would be easy, fulfilling, and needed (an example of a high score would be a relaxing shower). He suggests to try to eliminate, as much as possible, anything scoring lower than 25 (although some things, such as doing one's taxes, can be very difficult, highly unfulfilling, yet still necessary enough to compel us to do them). Several pages of charts with assorted activities are provided for the reader to score their lives with, and an area to total things up. A 10-point plan for disengaging from the low-scoring activities follows, with special attention (a couple of dozen specific sub-points) on dealing with assorted types of *Gemmelsmerch*.

The next part of this really surprised me. Hallowell passes along exercises from a Russian physical trainer who *"stresses that the most significant limits we have are the mental limits we impose on ourselves"* and insists on mental training as part of the physical regimen he puts his athlete students through. These are as simple as grids where one needs to point out the numbers 1-25 which are randomly distributed on 5x5 matrices and timing one's performance, to extremely difficult acts of concentration such as drawing different figures with both hands while tracing out others with one's feet! These reminded me somewhat of the sorts of things that various occult practitioners go through in training, which is hardly what I had expected in a book I thought was about "simplifying" one's life. The remaining bits of the book are suggestions on how to get these approaches set into one's habits and daily life, and how a few rare corporate entities are using similar things in an attempt to transcend the "standard" business grind and the blinders that come with it.

Needless to say, I was quite pleased to have discovered CrazyBusy[3], and I'm equally pleased to report that it (in a paperback edition) is still available, so should be obtainable via your local bookstore, but the hard-cover version I found at the dollar store can be had via the Amazon new/used guys for as little as 1¢ (plus shipping) for a "very good" copy. If you live your life *"Overstretched, Overbooked, and About to Snap"* like I do, this is likely a very useful thing for you to pick up!

Notes:
1. http://btripp-books.livejournal.com/89963.html
2-3. http://amzn.to/1SNENr8

Sunday, March 14, 2010[1]

So, you wanna be in pictures?

This was yet another book provided to me by its publisher, the good folks at Wiley (yes, FTC goons, I got a *review copy* so that I could *review* the book ... how *scandalous*!), which was "added on" to a book I'd requested. Long-time readers of this space will no doubt have a sense that "business" books are *not* in the top 50% of my reading preferences, but recently much of what I've been plowing through has been in the "job search" arena, and specifically the "new media" niche, a result of the writing I've been doing for The Job Stalker[2] blog over on the Chicago Tribune's "Chicago Now" blogging site. For books that I feature there, I do a brief introduction (largely directing folks to come over here for the *review*) along with an "interview" which is fairly constant book-to-book. This is the *first* time that I've had an author "beat me to the punch" and get the responses to my 8-question form back to me *before* I got around to writing the review, so kudos to Steve Garfield for being on the ball like that! More to the point, I was having a *very* hard time putting Get Seen: Online Video Secrets to Building Your Business[3] into context, and one point he made in his responses greatly clarified this for me ... the book is intended to be *a textbook*, and not so much a "popular read". The reason that this is an important point is that the text is very "blocky" with chunks of information, interviews, lists of equipment and resources, repeating over and over through the various sections. What seemed to be a very odd choice of format for a "book about online video" makes much more sense as being the core document for a 8-section *class* about online video!

The sections here are "Choosing a Camera", "Lighting and Sound", "Making Videos Without a Video Camera", "Recording and Shooting", "Editing", "Uploading", "Broadcast Live", and "Video Blogging" (with an additional section of interviews/profiles of a couple of dozen notables in the field). Each of these includes a collection of background information, "how to" elements, resources, interviews, screen captures, notes and commentary, all in a less-than-poetic flow of material. As noted, I launched into this without knowing its intent as a "text book" and found the structure off-putting, but each section is rich with information (I have many pages bookmarked here, all for things of the "hey I could use that info" sort, rather than "I need to quote that in my review"). I have already recommended Get Seen[4] to associates of mine who are experimenting with web video. Obviously, if one is already doing a lot of online video content, much of this book will be "additional resources" rather than "aha!" moments, but for somebody that is looking at moving beyond sending grainy phone-vids to Facebook, this would be a very good place to start (as long as they understood that this was *instruction* and not so much *literature*)!

What's probably the most useful element here is how the various bits are integrated, while they *read* as haphazard, the concepts and information are arrayed in a complicated dance, matching equipment and ideas with interviews of people who are using them, and how they are achieving their results, *why* they do what they do, etc., and once one is done with a section, one has a very good sense of what that is about and how one might go about putting these things into practice. I did find something irritating here, however ... although it is an unavoidable aspect to having a print book addressing an electronic subject, there are lots and lots and lots of links, nearly every point covered in the book is footnoted to a URL and, as one is sitting there reading it, there's no way to take advantage of them! If ever a book cried out to be a "hyperbook" on the web (where all the video would be a click away as well), it would be Get Seen[5] ... what's integral to this book is what the various e-readers should be aspiring to, but it's beyond the Kindle, beyond the Nook, beyond the iPad ... maybe Microsoft with the Courier[6] will "get it right" and provide the sort of platform that would make e-reading a book with as much potential content/link involvement as is in play here.

Needless to say, this being "hot off the presses", it should be available pretty much anywhere. Amazon has it at 34% off (less than the *used* guys!), so that might be your best bet. Again, this isn't a "casual read", but has a ton of info in it for those looking for a manual for getting started with web video.

Notes:

1. http://btripp-books.livejournal.com/90126.html
2. http://bit.ly/4JYua5
3-5. http://amzn.to/1YSxtsT
6. http://www.mobilemag.com/2010/03/06/microsoft-courier-video-leaked-the-ipad-killer/

Tuesday, March 16, 2010[1]

It's Greek to me ...

This was one of those books that was described in *another* book in glowing terms and that I just *had* to track down. I'm not 100% sure what the referring book was, but I believe it was one those books on Sion and the Jesus blood line ... and I was somewhat expecting this to have been more substantially connected to that genre than it is. As it turns out, Peter Kingsley's In the Dark Places of Wisdom[2] has almost *nothing* to do with that area of investigation, with the sole exception that the peoples involved in this had a colony in what is currently Marseilles, France (which is, of course, where the Magdalene and her daughter Sarah sought sanctuary). Unfortunately, this means that I spent the whole book with one part of my brain waiting for this particular theme to pop up!

No, this does not concern itself *at all* with that investigative niche, but is a look at something *almost* as arcane. The subject here is pre-Socratic Greek philosophy, and how the Athenians (especially Plato, it would appear) "screwed things up", replacing what had been *the love of Wisdom* with *the love of arguing about Wisdom*, and thus setting up Western Culture with a generally non-spiritual intellectual system.

The book is oddly composed, reading almost like a fire-side story, with most character and concept introductions presented at the end of long drawn out tellings of things. The main actors are a Greek people living in Asia Minor called the Phocaeans, who were said to be great seafarers and explorers, and closely related to the people of Samos, from whence Pythagoras came. In the sixth century BCE the Persian empire expanded to the coast, and the Phocaeans took to their ships and *left* spreading out to various colonies around the Mediterranean, among which was the city of Velia, another coastal spot, located towards the southern end of the west side of Italy.

Over the past 50 years or so, much interesting archaeological work has been done at the site of Velia, which appears to be the home of the philosopher Parmenides, founder of the "Eleatic" school, and teacher to the philosopher Zeno made famous by Plato's writings. He was also a priest of Apollo, and what the author describes as a *Phôlarchos*, which appears to mean something like "lord of the lair", with "lair" implying something like a bear's hibernation cave. The author connects this, much as in the manner of Orphic or Delphic visionary practices, to a shamanic tradition that involved the elect going into a pit under the shrine or temple and lying still there for extended periods (somewhat like various Native American tribes' "vision quest" practices) to become inspired by the deities.

Again, this is not an archaeological book, nor is it a linearly structured historical book, nor a work of specific philosophy, it unfolds like a long story being told, a myth spun out, and has the hazy bits that one would expect from those modes. The author evidently feels that there was a significant European shamanic wisdom tradition which expressed itself in the pre-Socratic (and progressively, pre-Platonic and pre-Aristotelian) Greek world, which was better, truer, and more whole than what has come down to us. Unfortunately, the dots don't quite connect here (this is, evidently, the first of a series of books, and it's supposedly *in the sequel* that the "real stuff" gets addressed!). Needless to say, between it not being about what I thought it was about when I got it, and it never quite "getting to the point" with any sort of an intellectual "payoff", this was a fairly frustrating read. It is interesting that it is published by "The Golden *Sufi* Center", which also leaves questions unanswered, as only very peripherally does anything "Sufi" come into this.

There *are* parts here which really have power, largely those where Kingsley is setting up his story early on:

> *What's missing is more powerful that what's there in front of our eyes. We all know that. The only trouble is that the missingness is too hard to bear, so we invent things to miss in our desperation. They are all only temporary substitutes. The world fills us with substitute after substitute and tries to convince us that nothing is missing. But nothing has the power to fill the hollowness we feel inside, so we have to keep replacing and modifying the things we invent as our emptiness throws its shadow over our life.*

and ...

> *The only difference between us and the mystics is that they learn to face what we find ways of running away from. That's the reason why mysticism has been pushed to the periphery of our culture: because the more we feel that nothingness inside us, the more we feel the need to fill the void.*

I only wish the book hadn't been such a tease. Sure, I know a lot more today about early Greek philosophical schools than I had before, but it toys with the reader more than I like. I also never got a good explanation on one thing that had stood out ever since the book arrived ... the spine has a sun-on-the horizon photo that is *upside down* ... I can't believe that it's a printing error, so I kept looking for "what it meant", but the best I can come up with is that it's a metaphor for the shamanic underworld and the Apollonic sun entering "the dark places of wisdom". Again the book leaves that hanging, like so much else in the text.

If <u>In the Dark Places of Wisdom</u>[3] sounds like something you'd love to get into (and there are certainly very appealing aspects to this), it appears to still be in print, and has a very low cover price (which Amazon has a discount that makes it about on a par with where the used guys have it, so that's probably your best bet, unless you hit a good sale at your local brick-and-mortar). While this does have a take-away of a long night chat session with your stoned Philosophy PhD buddy (who would no doubt find great meaning in the passage: *"The noise of a **syrinx** is the ultimate password. It's the sound of silence."* and want to dig deep into your record collection to prove some point), it is generally engaging and taught me a few things, so might be something you'd want to consider.

Notes:

1. http://btripp-books.livejournal.com/90603.html

2-3. http://amzn.to/1qRkzAf

Monday, March 22, 2010[1]

More at "encyclopedia" ...

This is another book provided to me by Wiley for review (helllooo FTC) ... they certainly seem to be in the forefront of the publishing wave on this particular niche! <u>Social Media 101: Tactics and Tips to Develop Your Business Online</u>[2] is the latest from Chris Brogan, the "Social Media guru" whose *Trust Agents* I wrote about a few weeks back. I've been following Chris on Twitter for quite a while (@ChrisBrogan) and have been reading his blog (http://www.chrisbrogan.com) a bit as well. This book is primarily a collection of 87 of his blog posts (edited and sequenced, etc., of course) which covers a wide span of material.

The book is sort of tricky ... first of all, it's *small* (slightly over 5x7", but thick at 350 pages), with a "cutesy" vintage clip art cover ... it *looks* like it's going to be a quick, fun read ... a perception reinforced by the short *chapters* (the blog posts) inside. Instead, it's like the proverbial "taking a drink from a firehose". Each of the 87 sections is a dense, tight, concise look at a particular angle of Social Media, and this is not what one can (if giving it appropriate attention) just breeze through!

As I've previously noted, when reading a book, I keep a bit of scrap paper (typically a cash register receipt) in the book to give me something to pull strips of paper from to "bookmark" places in what I'm reading, either for passages that I'm likely to want to use in a review, or information that I'm going to want to revisit at some point. I don't recall *ever* having more of these poking out of the top than there are in <u>Social Media 101</u>[3]. As those of you who read my personal blog know, I've worked a bit in the Social Media field and am currently in a job search which certainly includes this area. Brogan provides *dozens* of resources, lists, observations, etc. here that I *had to* mark to come back to. Unfortunately (for you), there don't seem to be any "Oh, I *must* include this passage in the review!" markers ... but chalk that up to each bit of this book being very focused on-topic, a side effect of it being an aggregation of compact, targeted blog entries!

However, these same attributes make this somewhat difficult to approach as a reviewer. Hardly being a "101" course in the subject of Social Media this is more like a non-alphabetized *encyclopedia* on the subject, circa late 2009ce. I really can't think of *anything* that's been left out of this ... with the one caveat that this is a *business* book and so the material constantly gravitates to that end of the spectrum. Again, there are 87 "chapters" here, so I'm not going to do a run-down of them, but the following are a "cherry picking" from the Contents listing: "Social Media Does Not Replace Marketing Strategy", "Using Social Networking Offline", "Participation: The Key to Social Media", "Social Media Starter Pack" (with five following sections and later industry-specific ones), "A Sample Blogging Work Flow", "Growing

Your Audience: Some Basics", "The Value of Networks", "The Sound of Content Ripping Free from Its Page", "What I Want a Social Media Expert to Know", "100 Personal Branding Tactics Using Social Media", "How to Do More with Less Time", and "How I Do It".

Of course, everything in here has to be considered a "snapshot" in time, as the field of Social Media is undergoing constant, rapid growth. As Chris notes at one point, it's also not been around for long enough to really have left a serious track on people resumes (at least in its current manifestations), so what's true today might not be true tomorrow. Except, of course, for the "basics", the "playing nice with the other children" stuff of being open, transparent, and useful. However, it's all in here. As I noted, I've worked in Social Media to various extents for the past couple of years, and, on one level, this really *makes my brain hurt* ... there is so much interwoven in this book that it's amazing that any one guy could know it all, and in the detail that Brogan evidently does. It's an impressive document, and indispensable for anybody looking to come to grips with the wider Social Media sphere, especially as it relates to businesses.

Social Media 101[4] is new, hot, and only been out for a month at this point, so you should be able to find a copy any place they have business books (hint: if you follow Chris' Twitter you'll hear of locations he's dropped in to and signed copies, such as on various airport concourses, etc.). Amazon has it at about 1/3rd off of cover, however, which makes it pretty reasonable. If you want to "look under the hood" on Social Media (or have a supervisor who needs to learn about it!), this is definitely the manual *du jour*.

Notes:

1. http://btripp-books.livejournal.com/90703.html
2-4. http://amzn.to/1QmMUVa

Sunday, March 28, 2010[1]

Something "catchy" ...

The concept of a "viral" expansion is very common in the world of the Internet (although I'm not so sure how well established it is in the quasi-Luddite worlds which aren't obsessively online), with things like videos (often inexplicably) suddenly bursting from well-deserved obscurity to attain millions of views from every corner of the planet. Those in the web professionally have spent a lot of mental energy trying to figure out the how/why/what dimensions of this, and, of course, marketers have invested large sums of money to try to replicate this sort of attention for projects featuring their products and services!

An associate of mine (whose site I helped build from a loose collection of "niche" web presences floating around on free web hosts to a social media platform in the Alexa 100k last summer), gave me a copy of Adam L. Penenberg's Viral Loop: From Facebook to Twitter, How Today's Smartest Businesses Grow Themselves[2] to help me come to grips on some of the issues we were having to deal with in relation to that project (like "How could we have so much traffic and user minutes but so little ad revenue?").

In this the concept of "viral" is directly addressed, which expresses itself mathematically as a "viral coefficient", which is how many people one person will introduce the site, product, or concept to ... a figure below 1 indicates low growth, a figure of 1 has slow growth, eventually stalling, but something that has a coefficient above 1 will eventually exhibit exponential growth, with figures as low a 1.2 quickly exploding up the graphs.

This is not, however, a math book. It is, frankly, more of a history of companies which have (or have not) had this sort of growth. One is tempted to think this has been solely a product of the Internet Age, but the near-instantaneous global reach has only super-charged the underlying functions of viral growth, and the book reflects this by first looking at companies like Tupperware in the 50's, and even to the somewhat related model created by the notorious Charles Ponzi in 1919/20. Of course, the dynamics which drove the growth of these examples found extreme expression when the Web came into the equation, and the book looks at many who won, lost, and rode assorted waves (it is amazing how many of these companies have been developed serially by a core group of entrepreneurs).

The dynamics of companies that have "gone viral" are picked apart here, and the concept of a "viral loop" introduced ... of particular interest is this list of "Shared Characteristics of Viral Loop Companies": *Web-based ... Free ... Organizational technology ... Simple concept ... Build-in virality ... Extremely fast adoption ... Exponential growth ... Virality index ... Predictable growth rates ... Network effects ... Stackability ... Point of nondisplacement ... Ultimate saturation.* Obviously, most of these concepts need the level of explanation that's given in the book (for instance, "Stackability" is the way that one viral company can piggyback on another, in the way that PayPal grew through the already viral eBay), so I won't try to even thumbnail all of those here.

Again, while there is quite a lot of *theory* in Viral Loop[3], the examples are always anchored to specific companies, and individuals, so this phases back and forth between a book about virality in general, and a historical document (having *lived through the early evolution of the Web* myself, I found it fascinating to "have a program" with all the players and their roles detailed!) which tracks the development of the viral model over the past couple of decades. Social media (much covered in this space of late) is only the latest manifestation of what these dynamics produce, and it's interesting to ponder where this all will be going next.

Viral Loop[4] is a relatively recent release (last year), so it's likely to be available at your local brick-and-mortar book vendor if they have much business or internet product available. Amazon has it at about 1/3rd off of cover, and the new/used guys have new copies that you could get for under ten bucks (including shipping), so it's pretty painlessly available. If you have a more professional or technical interest in things in the Social Media sphere, this is likely something that you should be adding to your "to be read" pile!

Notes:
1. http://btripp-books.livejournal.com/90918.html
2-4. http://amzn.to/1SNB9hd

Sunday, March 28, 2010[1]

Not the end of the world?

Here's another deal snagged from that B&N.com after-after-after-holiday sale ... which is sort of a two-for-one, as it's both something of a comedy book, *and* it's something that I can feature in *The Job Stalker*[2] as a career book! Such a deal. Now, as I've pointed out previously, getting stuff for $2/copy tends to eliminate some filters, and, generally speaking, these books are not things that I *sought out*, so going in on them I don't have any major expectations, so it's a bonus when I find myself being enthusiastic about one of these, after the reading.

Fired!: Tales of the Canned, Canceled, Downsized, and Dismissed[3] is listed as being "written and edited" by Annabelle Gurwitch, but this is primarily a collection of other people's stories, so I get the impression that "collected and edited" would probably be closer to the truth, except for the section she contributes on her own experiences, and the introductory essays (and, I suppose the identifying paragraphs that follow most of the 55 entries).

This is, as one could gather from the subtitle, the stories of people who have been *fired* from various jobs, covering a wide array of situations from high-profile editorial posts to the unhappy characters who got fired mere *hours* into menial jobs. Gurwitch is an actress/writer and most of the tales here were evidently collected through entertainment industry contacts. There are a few "famous" names adding tales of their career mishaps ... Bill Maher, Tim Allen, Bob Saget, Harry Shearer, and even non-comics such as Robert Reich (Secretary of Labor in the Clinton administration).

Most of these are reminiscences of youthful false-starts, although a few are about very visible public flame-outs (such as Saget's getting pushed off the CBS *Morning Program*), and being fired by the truly famous (Gurwitch's own termination by her idol, Woody Allen, or an ad agency gal who managed to be fired by Leona Helmsley *three times*). They range from one-page e-mail responses to five-page essays, with a couple of interviews, a *recipe*, and even a *song* (with full sheet music).

The book is organized in five sections, "The Job So Terrible You Can Only Hope to Be Fired", "The Firing You Didn't See Coming", "The Time You Deserved to Be Fired", "The Time Getting Fired Leads You to Something Better", and "The Time You Had to Fire Yourself" ... with a dozen or so pieces in each, giving the book something of a flow (as opposed to the "type" of firing being randomly distributed through the book). However, one added piece serves to give this a slight whiff of gravitas, a "fired fact" add-on to most of these, which serves to put some hard numbers to trends drifting through the stories. Here's one head-scratcher from these:

> *Percentage of workers satisfied with their jobs earning less than $15,000 a year: 17.*

> *Percentage of workers satisfied with their jobs earning more than $50,000 a year: 14.*
>
> *Percentage of workers who would like to fire their boss: 20.*

Because on one level Fired![4] is somewhat of an "insiders joke" for the entertainment industry, the humor used can get a bit raunchy, best exemplified by the *awesome* line in Dana Gould's piece: *"Over the years I had my hand in more pilots than an Air Force proctologist."* ... showing the wit that eventually landed him a job as a writer/producer with *The Simpsons*.

As one might expect, given the bargain price at which I obtained my hardcover copy, this particular edition of Fired![5] is out of print, although available from the new/used guys for as little as a penny used and as little as a buck new ... but it's also now in a paperback reprint via BN.com (Amazon doesn't seem to list that one). If you're looking for a way to help yourself or a friend through an "involuntary separation" experience, this could be a great way to raise the spirits. This is no earthshaking tome of career revelations, but it is a very interesting and engaging look at how many people (several quite familiar) had to deal with these sort of challenges!

Notes:

1. http://btripp-books.livejournal.com/91143.html
2. http://bit.ly/4JYua5
3-5. http://amzn.to/1MXjscF

Saturday, April 3, 2010[1]

Utopia ...

As I have frequently mentioned in this space, I've been a great fan of the Dover Thrift Editions books ... largely as a vehicle for getting a just-under-$25 order up into the free shipping promised land. They also tend to be relatively short, which certainly helps with keeping up on my "72 non-fiction books a year" quest, especially in months where my other reading is either lengthy or dense (or something that I'm reading more "out of duty", such as the business books that have passed through here of late, rather than "out of love"). The "nobler" benefit of the Dover books is that I'm able to "plug holes" in my education ... filling in lapses where I'd read *of* something but hadn't actually ever gotten around to *reading* it.

Sir Thomas More's Utopia[2] is a very good example of this, of course. A classic of English literature (although it was originally written in Latin), it is nearly 500 years old at this point, penned as a satire, primarily of the government (and reign) of Henry VIII. At this remove, the book suffers somewhat in that the modern reader (unless one is an enthusiast for that period of history) has only the thinnest context in which to frame the content, and what might have been acute barbs in 1515 are unlikely to even be recognized as sardonic salvos today.

The bulk of the book is a tale told by a traveler, one that More claims to have encountered while in Europe. The first part of the book is More describing his business there, and the various personages with whom he had contact, including one who introduces him to this traveler. The first part is rather hard to follow, being (I take it) more "setting the table" with a discourse of current views and attitudes, and features arguments from various positions. Frankly, not being much of a fan of either fiction or philosophy, there were several places here where it just became "blah, blah, blah" to me, and I wondered when the "travel book" was going to kick in. Obviously, this is more a failing on my part than on More and his book's, but the format was (to a modern eye) rather dissonant in several aspects.

Of course, the book would not have the fame it has were it not for the titular land, Utopia. This had been visited by the traveler, and the second part of the book is his relating his impressions and recall of the place and its people. It is pretty evident that Marx, Engels, etc. had read this in the course of developing their ideas, as much of what is presented as the Utopian way would sound very familiar to anyone listening to a Progressive agitator. The term "Utopia" comes from Greek roots suggesting "nowhere", and so the concept of this "ideal society" is unobtainable in the real world. Again, how this relates to Henry VIII and his government, I can't specifically say!

I found it interesting that, among all the *fantasy* names that More gives to the Utopians' world, the name of their main God is easily recognizable ...

Mithras. As More ended up being executed for opposing Henry VIII's take-over of the English church, there must be something quite pointed in this usage, but, again at the remove of time and context from which I'm reading this, it only serves as a titillating clue for possible future consideration.

It is fascinating how much of what is attributed to the Utopians seems very familiar from the past century of our culture. While much of what they are presented as doing still seems quite odd to us, it must have been wholly bizarre to More's contemporaries. I'd be very interested in hearing how Leftist voices view this book, as certainly much of their idealized programs have echoes in Utopia ... it is enticing to try to pick apart how much of Marx (and perhaps even *Jefferson*) might have been lifted from More's fantasy. There are several points which resonate with the Libertarian cause as well, so the vision here is hardly just a paleo-socialist screed.

Anyway, as this *is* a Dover Thrift Edition, Utopia[3] is remarkably inexpensive in this version (which is a reprint of an 1885 edition) , with a *cover price* of just $2.00 ... which makes it ideal for those on-line order situations where one has two books and a buck and change to make up to get up to free shipping!

Notes:

1. http://btripp-books.livejournal.com/91411.html

2-3. http://amzn.to/2345M1h

Sunday, April 11, 2010[1]

A beautifully written book ...

One of the downsides of much of the reading that I do, and especially in the reading that I *recently* have been doing, is that the writing involved is functional, pedestrian, and *bland*. Of course, one would hardly *demand* "high art" out of a book focused on the job search, but the lack of beautifully composed prose in most of these came into harsh light of late, light emanating from A. (Alfred) Alvarez's The Writer's Voice[2]. This was one of those books that I had picked up via BN.com's after-after-after-holiday sale for two bucks, and was picked (as I've mentioned at length previously) more on the basis of *"oh, this sounds like it might be interesting"* rather than any particular focused intent on the book or its author.

Alvarez "is a poet, novelist, literary critic, anthologist, and author of many highly praised books" (according to the dust jacket), but I'd never encountered him previously. The book is based on a series of lectures that he presented at the New York Public Library in 2002 on "Finding a Voice", "Listening", and "The Cult of Personality and the Myth of the Artist".

Again, the main take-away that I had from this was the quality of the prose, and as I read through the book I marked various pages which held "choice nuggets" exemplifying this. Rather than trying to summarize the gist of the three lectures, I'll attempt to string together these quotes to give you some sense of why I found this so special.

Interestingly, the book starts with, and eventually returns to, psychoanalysis, with Alvarez comparing the writer's search for "their voice" with an individual's inner struggles. He spends a goodly amount of time looking at Sigmund Freud, who he notes to have been unusually artistic in his literary output.

> {Speaking of Freud:}
>
> *The mystery, of course, is that of the unconscious – how things we don't know about ourselves soak through like rising damp, changing what we think we know and how we behave.*

Obviously, there's the poet's voice coming through here ... phrases of the caliber of "soak through like rising damp" somehow missed the page in those Social Media books I've been reading! He sets up the psychological argument, and then back-tracks into literature, analyzing the various modes of different eras.

> {Regarding Shakespeare:}
>
> *In one form or another, linguistic ostentation is the*

> *fuel that drives the play {Love's Labors Lost} forward and all parties are equally immodest. The difference is one of tone and manners – the courtier versus the pendant, elegance and edge versus braggadocio and vacuous circumlocution.*

And, who of us has *not* been guilty of "vacuous circumlocution" at one time or another (albeit not necessarily labeled as such at the time)? Alvarez works his way through the years until reaching the modern era, and comes up with some choice bits about the difference between poetry and prose:

> {Discussing Plath:}
> *No matter how many times you rewrite prose or how easily it seems to read when you are done with it, prose is never quite finished. There is always a word ill-chosen or out of place, a repetition you missed, an adjective that could be cut, a comma that should have been a semicolon – something to set your teeth on edge when you reread it later in cold print. Poems don't work like that. They are as intricate as the giant locks on a bank vault: each one of the dozens of tumblers has to click into place before the door will swing open.*

That is superb, and every writer whose works have found their way into "cold print" can certainly identity with the frustrations outlined in this passage. This is part of an interesting discussion of modes of writing poetry, that of the "carver" and the "modeler", and how Sylvia Plath started out as one but, in her last tragic burst of creativity, became the latter.

In the "listening" section, Alvarez reaches out into other areas, including popular music. The focus here is that, for a writer to find his or her "voice", there must be readers out there who have developed the ability to actually "listen".

> {Analyzing Cole Porter's *"I Get A Kick Out of You"*:}
> *The stunning final image opens the door, as it were, onto the stunning melody, yet the lines that lead up to it are curiously slack and low-key – a chatty recitative, a deliberately nonchalant meander towards revelation, as if the singer were clearing his throat before he bursts into song.*

One wonders how long the author spent crafting the line "a deliberately nonchalant meander towards revelation" which strikes my ear the way some morsel of exquisite culinary skill would hit my palate! Again, finding a book that speaks this way, quite by happenstance, has proven a most appreciated treat (and respite from the "business books" that I now find myself frequently the recipient of).

In the final lecture, he turns to the *idea* of the writer/artist in society (and changing notions of this role over time), and comes up with some rather arch observations. The following particularly got my attention, as it so closely parallels both my *technique* for writing back when I was producing 250 poems a year, *and* the reasons that I had to quit writing.

> {Arguing against D.H. Lawrence:}
>
> *I myself believe that this is the exact opposite of the truth: you don't shed your sicknesses, you dredge them up in writing and thereby make them readily available to you, so that you find yourself living them out. Nature, that is, always imitates art, usually in a sloppy and exaggerated way.*

"You find yourself living them out", which for me was a NLP-like feedback loop of dredged-up anguish, dread, and angst that (by the act of "materializing" them as words on paper) fed back into my psyche as the "real" reality.

Anybody who writes, or appreciates *writing* would get a lot from The Writer's Voice[3], as well as those with an interest in psychiatry, cultural trends, and the history of literature. I can't recall a book that I quite so *enjoyed* reading for well-crafted passages like those quoted here. I would highly recommend this to all and sundry!

Despite it getting into my hands via a clearance sale, this does seem to still be in print. It's part of the Norton Lecture series, so I suspect that it has an audience in the academic market. However, the new/used guys have "like new" copies for as little as 1¢ (plus shipping), which might be your best bet if you're not up for parting with the $21.95 cover price. Not that this isn't *worth* that (even for a fairly slim volume), of course. Highly recommended!

Notes:

1. http://btripp-books.livejournal.com/91836.html
2-3. http://amzn.to/1SNbXHE

Sunday, April 11, 2010[1]

Your mileage may vary ...

Like my just-reviewed book by A. Alvarez, this was obtained via the $2 sale at BN.com, but this exhibits a different end result ... where I *might not* have purchased the other in a store (and missed its pleasures), I'm reasonably sure that, given the chance to flip through this, I would have been very *unlikely* to have picked it up. Now, this is not to say that Ethical Ambition: Living a Life of Meaning and Worth[2] by Prof. Derrick Bell is not a *good* book, it certainly is that, it's just that it's based on realities sufficiently outside of my experience to require acts of contextual identification beyond what I'm in the habit of attempting.

Prof. Bell was the first Black member of the Harvard Law School faculty, has held various positions in the Justice Department, been very active with the NAACP, and been on the faculties of several universities. From just reading this book, one gets the impression that he developed his biggest notoriety from assorted protests involving his highly-visible professional positions, which led him to take unpaid leaves or quit what most would consider to be cushy much-to-be-maintained tenured situations in the name of some "issue" or another which he felt needed to be highlighted.

Obviously, the title "Ethical Ambition" comes from this, and on some level the book seems to be his putting his resume in the framework of doing what he felt needed to be done at these various points in his life. As much as I typically avoid "philosophy" books, this is one case where I had really hoped for a more abstracted work. Unfortunately (at least from the standpoint of my connecting with it), this is very much grounded in "the Black experience" and the "civil rights" movement ... cultural elements of which I am (at best) an outside observer.

The book is in six chapters, each dealing with a different area of ethical concern: "The Power In Passion", "Courage and Risk Taking", "Evolving Faith", "Advancing Relationships", "Ethical Inspiration", and "Humility's Wisdom". The book started out strongly enough, with the first two chapters being things easily generalized, but somewhat "fell off the table" after that.

Here's a snippet from the second chapter:

> Courage is a decision you make to act in a way that works through your own fear for the greater good as opposed to pure self-interest. Courage means putting at risk your immediate self-interest for what you believe is right. The stakes don't have to be life and death, and the situation doesn't have to be dramatic. You could exercise courage in a conversation were the greatest risk you run is being yelled at, laughed at, or refused.

And, here's a bit from the fourth:

> For some of us, it is easier to confront an angry boss or even a hostile crowd than it is to leave an exciting work project and do justice as a spouse and parent. Achieving balance in an ongoing challenge, but an absolutely necessary one, and one well worth the continuing effort it requires.

Again, this is not so much a *philosophical* book as it is a quasi-autobiography in which the author tries to frame certain issues and life challenges in relation to his experiences. Personally, I don't think he achieved a level of detaching the ethical theory implied in these chapters from the specifics of his own experience, or from the thrust of his career. In order to get some context, I did what I rarely do and peeked at some other reviews ... interestingly it seems that this books is required reading for 1st year law students at some schools (those I'd guess with strong "civil rights" programs) ... there seemed to be two themes of thought on this, unbridled enthusiasm from those of a progressive bent, and folks brushing this off as pure ego-inflation (*"arrogance and vanity seeping off the pages"*) on Bell's part.

I'm certainly willing to cut Prof. Bell slack on having a self-focused book, but then the question becomes *"what's the book for?"*, as it speaks of ethical situations grounded in rather narrow contexts, which he then struggles to make more universal statements about. The passages quoted above were extracted from text which dealt with very specific events. I, of course, have no idea how this came to print, but (from having been in the publishing biz) can imagine a tug-of-war between the author and his editors to make this more about "Living a Life of Meaning and Worth" than "my struggles with ethics and bad people who just don't get it" ("my struggles" could have made a snappy title, albeit causing certain problems in some foreign editions).

Anyway, I am very likely not the "key audience" for Ethical Ambition[3] and how you'll like it will depend (I believe) on your politics and cultural milieu. Bell at least seems to *try* to make some universal statements about ethics, but does seem bogged down by both ego and mission. I certainly wouldn't recommend spending *full cover price* for this (it is out there discounted, no doubt for the academic market), but if it does sound like something you'd be interested in, the new/used guys on Amazon have "like new" copies for as little as a penny (four bucks with shipping). Definitely a "your mileage may vary" case.

Notes:

1. http://btripp-books.livejournal.com/92079.html
2-3. http://amzn.to/1qQES0w

Sunday, April 18, 2010[1]

An essential for the job search ...

As I've alluded to in this space before, my reviewing of books has suddenly become noted in certain sectors, obviously due to my having been penning the Chicago Tribune's "Chicago Now" site's _The Job Stalker_[2] blog over the past six months or so. The current book, however, was the first instance of a contact made by the publisher's promotional arm _to me_ about a book, rather than coming from my querying _them_ about a review copy! So, for the FTC and others who might care, this represents a copy sent to me by the good folks at the Portfolio division of the Penguin Group.

Use Your Head to Get Your Foot in the Door: Job Secrets No One Else Will Tell You[3] is the latest release from the "best selling author" of _Swim With The Sharks_ (among others), Harvey Mackay, who appears to be an interesting case ... a business man who has developed a booming side-line in speaking, writing, and syndicated columns, while still maintaining his core business, an envelope manufacturing company. Perhaps it is this which prompts him to offer a "Get a Job or Get Your Money Back Guarantee", which promises to refund the book's purchase price if you follow his advice but still aren't employed within six months!

As long-time readers will appreciate (and as I've kvetched about previously), I am not a _fan_ of business books, career management books, or job-search books, but have been thrust by circumstances largely beyond my control (my third major job search in ten years), to have become very conversant in this particular niche. So, it was without any significant enthusiasm that I launched into reading the current volume. Despite this, I was soon won over by Mr. Mackay's style, and his approach to presenting his information.

Use Your Head to Get Your Foot in the Door[4] is broken into eight major sections, from "Dark Days" to "Stay Afloat" (which comes after "Get Hired"), and these are broken down into numerous sub-sections each addressing key points. The book is sprinkled with cartoons from the _New Yorker_ magazine, as well as "Quickie" one-page sidebars which highlight specific suggestions (such as "The Lecture Room in your Laptop" which directs readers to resources such as the TED talks, as well as universities, such as MIT and Yale, which have put courses up for free on the web).

It is hard to briefly cover this book, as there is _so much in it_, a truly staggering amount of information on a wide array of topics related to the job search. Again, its main structure in walking the reader through an experiential timeline from becoming unemployed through getting a new job, with pieces that suggest they started out as free-standing columns, plus interviews, stories, "coaching" and _lists_. The author is clearly quite fond of lists, and they range from the "Ten Reasons to Buy This Book" up before the table of contents to the "Lucky 13" list[5] of recommended books in the "Afterthoughts" section. Frankly, some of the best bits of this book are in those lists, like "The Mackay 22" which is a "debriefing" run-down for you to fill out immediately after any interview (and its more "basic" predecessor, the "Mackay 44" which is a pre-interview checklist), and the famed (I guess, I'd not heard of it previously, but this stuff isn't my core competency) "Mackay 66" contact management system (the forms for which are downloadable at his website[6]).

As mentioned above, I'm in my *third* job search in the past decade, and I have used numerous "career management" groups, "career counselors", "career services", "career centers" and read more job-search/career books than I have ever wanted, and have *never* encountered a more encyclopedic system for getting a job than this book. While it is an easy, diverse read, it is constantly focused on the realities of the job search, and is up-to-the-moment as far as technology and the current economic realities are concerned. I have picked up *dozens* of "I did *not* know that!" points here, ranging from government programs I'd never heard of, to on-line resources that I'd managed to miss in my own wanderings through the Internet, to the various useful features like the above-detailed lists. While I'm certainly going to be incorporating elements of Mackay's system in my own job search, I'd *highly* recommend this to anybody faced with having to find a job.

Since Mackay is a top-selling author an this is brand new, it's pretty much a sure bet that you'll be able to find Use Your Head to Get Your Foot in the Door[7] at your local brick-and-mortar bookseller, although Amazon currently has it at 34% off of cover price. Again, even for somebody as battered and scarred from the job search wars as I am, this is a useful book, and it should be *the manual* for most everybody else heading into that fight!

Notes:

1. http://btripp-books.livejournal.com/92270.html
2. http://www.chicagonow.com/blogs/job-stalker/
3-4. http://amzn.to/1qQCTtg
5. http://www.chicagonow.com/blogs/job-stalker/2010/04/from-a-book-about-some-books.html
6. http://www.harveymackay.com/
7. http://amzn.to/1qQCTtg

Monday, April 26, 2010[1]

The earliest humans ...

As I've no doubt mentioned in this space previously, one of the perks of being a member of LibraryThing[2] is the ability to participate in their "Early Reviewer" program. While the available books each month are heavily weighted towards fiction, I find myself getting review copies of interesting books (of the non-fiction I prefer) every few months. I was rather pleased to have "scored" (via The Algorithm which matches books in your on-line library to the books you've requested) Brian Fagan's Cro-Magnon: How the Ice Age Gave Birth to the First Modern Humans[3], as I've not had a chance to read many Archaeology books of late, and certainly not in the pre-historic area.

As one can surmise from the sub-title, this book largely focuses on the Ice Age eras, covering a period from about 130,000 to about 10,000 years ago, and primarily dealing with sites in Europe. It also deals with two main Hominid species, typically called *Neanderthals* and *Cro-Magnons* (both of those names arising from dig sites where remains were found). Recent research has suggested that these two lines were different branches arising from a more ancient common ancestral species *Homo ergaster* which arose from *Homo habilis* and also spawned *Homo erectus*, all of these in Africa. The Neanderthals had moved out of Africa and into Europe by 200,000 years ago, which pre-dates the current estimate of the development of the Cro-Magnons, who were *Homo sapiens*. The first part of the book deals with what we know of the Neanderthals, which is limited by their extinction somewhere around 30,000 years ago. The author presents some interesting speculation as to how the Neanderthals lived, and what their inner and cultural life was like, in that it appears that they did not have much language, or an ability to abstract from the immediate (although they certainly were intelligent to be very effective hunters).

This brings me to a minor caveat about something that kept coming up for me in this book: much of it is comprised of "stories" or imagined scenarios, several borrowed from books of (pre-) historical fiction. While certainly making the end product more appealing than a running catalog of spear points and hearth layers, I found myself frequently asking *how do you know that?*, and not getting much in terms of solid, statistical, answers. This made the information flow more like walking through a museum's dioramas and taking what was presented as the main data, not unpleasant, not un-informative, but somehow lacking something.

However, this is not to say that Cro-Magnon[4] isn't chock-full of fascinating stuff ... it has one of the best descriptions of the "population bottleneck" that *Homo sapiens* went through 73,500 years ago. One of the amazing data points here is that modern Humans have *less genetic diversity* than is exhibited in chimpanzee troops in West Africa. How did this happen? The largest volcanic episode in the past *twenty-three million years*, the explosion of Mount Toba (in what is currently Sumatra), which threw the Earth into a nightmare of ash and cold and death. *Homo sapiens* had begun to move out of Africa as early as 100,000 years ago into the mid-east and other regions, but these were wiped out in the wake of the Toba eruption. In fact, extrapolating from the DNA evidence, there were perhaps as few as 10,000 humans that survived the aftermath.

It took another 20,000 or so years for human populations to get to the point where they were moving out of Africa again, and the first Cro-Magnons found their way to Europe about 45,000 years ago. Here they spread out in the ice-bound world (which the author constantly parallels with modern Arctic cultures for clues, cultural and technological) in competition with the surviving Neanderthals. There were various "cultural phases" (largely based on assorted tools, and their distribution), from the Neanderthal "Mousterian" which ranged from 100,000 to about 30,000 years ago, to the Cro-Magnon "Aurignacian", "Gravettian", "Solutrean", and the "Magdalenian" phases, which appeared from 40,000 to 11,000 years ago.

Another interesting piece presented here was that, for all that time, the Hominid diet was almost 100% meat-based, with the average individual not consuming "more than a cupful" of plant material in a given year. It wasn't until the post-Glacial era (about 10,000 years ago) that Europe changed from a frozen tundra to a heavily-forested landscape, and that "hunter-gatherer" lifestyle began to take hold. Another major shift happened with the onset of warmer temperatures, in the middle-east, what had been lush grasslands were turning to scrub, and the people there found that if there was going to be grass for their prey, they needed to plant seed, eventually developing into agriculture. From about 10,000 to 7,000 years ago, these farming people (the LBK culture) spread into Europe, existing side-by side with the now hunter-gatherer remnants of Magdalenian Cro-Magnon culture now existing in the forests. Eventually the farming culture absorbed the Cro-Magnon culture, although (through analysis of DNA markers), 85% of European genetic heritage has a Cro-Magnon basis.

One point the author comes back to repeatedly is that the Cro-Magnon peoples were, physically, intellectually, etc. identical to modern humans, and were bringing to bear on their challenges as much brain and will and emotion (and likely a good deal more brawn and agility) than their modern descendants do to ours.

Cro-Magnon[5] is not a technical book, but is quite an evocative look at our long-ago forebearers. This is not likely to end up a college textbook, but is a very interesting window into the history of our species, in that period where our ancestors were *becoming human*. As the book is brand new, it's a good bet that your local brick-and-mortar book seller will have it, although Amazon is featuring it at a rather substantial 34% discount.

Notes:
1. http://btripp-books.livejournal.com/92668.html
2. http://librarything.com/
3-5. http://amzn.to/1SN8hFR

Sunday, May 2, 2010[1]

If you want to get technical about it ...

Wow. Talk about a HOT topic. OK, so maybe not in *your* universe, but off in the Twitter-centric zone that I've been operating amid for the past couple of years the concept of measurement of marketing within the Social Media sphere is *huge*, with many agencies (several of which have been repeatedly subjected to my resume) strongly focused on this. Needless to say, Jim Sterne's Social Media Metrics: How to Measure and Optimize your Marketing Investment[2] is likely to cause quite a stir. This is another book in Wiley's "The New Rules of Social Media" series, which (like *Get Seen*, reviewed here previously) are volumes intended as *textbooks* for various aspects of the Social Media milieu. Of course, for the benefit of the FTC, I need to note that this was a *review copy* sent to me by Wiley ... however, I'm certainly glad they did, as this was a most fascinating read, and I would have been fairly unlikely to have picked this up as a "freerange" purchase.

This brings me to two things I should probably note about this book, it *is* somewhat textbook-like in its presentation, and it is very much a *business* book. It is not a light read and it really isn't for anybody who is uninvolved with the commerce of the new social internet. The author targets "the big three goals": 1 – increase revenue, 2 – lower costs, and 3 – improve customer satisfaction ... and he returns to these as touchstones throughout the book. As far as structure is concerned, the book is in nine chapters, each dealing with a particular aspect of the business use of Social Media: Getting Focused – Identifying Goals, Getting Attention – Reaching Your Audience, Getting Respect – Identifying Influence, Getting Emotional – Recognizing the Sentiment, Getting Response – Triggering Action, Getting the Message – Hearing the Conversation, Getting Results – Driving Business Outcomes, Getting Buy-in – Convincing Your Colleagues, and Getting Ahead – Seeing the Future.

Much like the previous book in this series that I've read, Social Media Metrics[3] just *screams* to be an e book, as it is chock-full of web material, either presented as screen captures or URLs. As much of a fan as I am of the "dead tree" model of data transfer, there were dozens of times while reading this that I wished I could *click on the page* and be whisked off to the material being referenced. Unfortunately, lacking this ability, I have a forest of small paper bookmarks rising out of the book, awaiting a few hours of leisure to manually make the transfer from ink-on-paper to the Internet!

As one can surmise from the progression of chapter headings above, this walks the reader from *almost* point zero (one would doubt that a total net newbie would pick up this book, and the author clearly shares this perception), with a definition of what Social Media is and in what forms it currently presents itself, through a very interesting list of "100 Ways to Measure Social Media", and into the various steps, from Awareness to Engagement to Persuasion to Conversion to Retention, which are necessary for achieving one's business' goals.

The author is also very clear that this is a "snapshot" in time ... referring to things that happened in the 90's as "last century", and being very direct that his examples are what's happening *now* amid an unending state of flux as new technologies, new players, new approaches, new realities all bubble up to the surface. That said, there are *dozens* of remarkably useful examples provided here, companies, programs, web resources, etc., etc. etc. that would provide the businessperson eager to forge a Social Media strategy with all the tools currently at hand for the purpose. Extremely useful is the "Resources" appendix which collects together (via URL and description) a wide range of papers and studies from major universities and cutting-edge marketing groups such as Zocalo, Razorfish, and Ogilvy's 360°.

I have already recommended Social Media Metrics[4] to several folks involved in this area (and told some Twitter folks that I'd seen them "name-checked" in here!), and that certainly goes for anyone reading this review. If you're looking to move beyond Social Media *as* Social Media and into the Business aspects of that market, this is *definitely* a book that you will want to check out. Again, this is a business book for business people, and is a textbook, not a "popular discussion", but if you're in the intended audience, you will get great benefit from picking this up.

As this is brand-new (it's officially been out for less than a month at this point), it *should* be available via your local brick-and-mortar book vendor (although, with this narrow a focus it might not be *everywhere*), but at the moment Amazon has it at a rather remarkable 45% off of cover, which is a hard deal to pass up ... if you're in "the Social Media business", this is something you're going to want to have at hand!

Notes:

1. http://btripp-books.livejournal.com/92800.html
2-4. http://amzn.to/1VURuAX

Sunday, May 2, 2010[1]

And now for something completely different ...

What can you really say about a book like On Guerrilla Warfare[2] by Mao Tse-tung? It has at least three things going against a broad discussion ... first, it is "a classic", generally placed in the same category as Sun Tzu, Clausewitz, etc., second, "we know how it came out" (the book itself is written mid-struggle against Imperial Japan) leading to speaking more about things *other than* the book when discussing it, and finally, it's not that much *of* a book, being fairly short and not very specific. This is almost a *philosophic* treatise, looking at how Guerrilla Warfare fits within various struggles (military, political, societal, etc.), rather than a *manual* dealing with the execution of a guerrilla campaign. A more *tactical* volume kept coming to mind while reading this, that being Abby Hoffman's *Steal This Book*, which is arguably more of a "guerrilla manual" than Mao's book. This is long on the over-all place of guerrilla actions within Mao's war, and short on "in situations like A, B, and C, you will likely want to set X number of charges at Y rail facilities, accompanied by Z distracting actions" (which would have made for a much more interesting book).

Instead, this talks of how guerrilla forces can be assembled, used in conjunction with standard armies, how they need to interface with the local peoples, and their utilization of existing geographies and situations. All of this is within the context of the war against the Japanese invaders of China. The book was initially written in 1937, and Mao's communist forces were just one element within the military and political spectrum. The introduction (written by translator Samuel B. Griffith of the USMC) notes that at this time Mao, although having obvious "bad intentions" towards them, was making a point of showing a "united front" with the Nationalist forces of Chiang Kai-shek and the book focuses primarily on the "liberation struggle" and less on the political front. It is interesting, however, to note (in the sections dealing with group organization) the importance given to "Political Officers", one of which was assigned to every command level.

The introduction is a key part of this book (taking up 1/3rd of its pages), having been initially written in 1940, just a few years after the book had been published in China, and it appears to have been an official Marine Corps analysis of Mao's book. Mr. Griffith later added, in 1961, further commentary, which put Mao's theoretical material into the context of eventual Chinese history, as well as looking at what developed in Cuba and Viet Nam.

One of the more evocative passages was when Mao was discussing the odds of success with guerrilla operations:

> *China is a country half colonial and half feudal; it is a country that is politically, militarily, and economi-*

> *cally backward. This is an inescapable conclusion. It is a vast country with great resources and tremendous population, a country in which the terrain is complicated and the facilities for communication are poor. All these factors favor a protracted war; they all favor the application of mobile warfare and guerrilla operations. ... Thus the time will come when a gradual change will become evident in the relative position of ourselves and our enemy, and when that day comes, it will be the beginning of our ultimate victory over the Japanese.*

Much of why the Chinese communists fell away from their Russian brethren arises in these perceptions; Mao understood that the China he was born into was not prepared for an *industrial* workers' uprising, but that the power had to come from the rural peasantry. The focus provided by the Japanese invasion allowed Mao and his cohorts to strip away the feudal and colonial influences, and create their own brand of communist regime.

On a personal note, I found a few things somewhat amusing about the book, on various levels. First, *within* the book, there are organizational charts and *Public Relations* departments are a major function, often with as many officers in place as the *intelligence* staff (hey, I could get *a job*!). I also found it amusing that (when I added this to my LibraryThing[3] collection) I discovered that I'd had a hard cover edition of this from back in the days of my reading a great deal of military history. And finally, I found it "interesting" that, of all the books that I'd ordered from the Barnes & Nobel after-after-after holiday sale, this was the only one (out of 13 books) that was shipped separately (hmmm ... did it have to get registered by Homeland Security before delivery?).

The present edition of On Guerrilla Warfare[4] is from Dover (although not one of their "thrift" editions), and has a fairly reasonable cover price (although I got this for under two bucks), so if you're thinking of getting this, you might want to keep it on the "bump up to $25" list, as paying shipping on the new/used guy's copies would take this pretty much up to cover anyway. This certainly is an interesting look at a particularly chaotic bit of world history, but if you're not particularly fascinated with that sort of material, this probably isn't for you.

Notes:

1. http://btripp-books.livejournal.com/93082.html
2. http://amzn.to/23412sC
3. http://btripp-books.com/
4. http://amzn.to/23412sC

Saturday, May 8, 2010[1]

Like hiring a career counselor, only cheaper ...

OK, right up front here I need to get this out: if this was a case and I was a *judge*, I'd probably have to recuse myself from hearing it, so I want readers to know that I had to *struggle* to a certain extent to give a fair review to this book. Why? Well, as long-time observers of this space may recall, I'm in the midst of my *third* major job quest in the past 10 years (one of the elements that landed me in The Job Stalker[2] blogging gig on the Tribune's "Chicago Now" site), and had used various "career management" groups and "job coaches" in my previous searches. None of these turned out well, and I have some significant emotional "sore spots" when dealing with elements of that industry. So, please bear with me when I find myself having to "tapdance" around certain points rather than go off on a rant about why X, Y, or Z don't work for *me*. Oh, and for our ever-vigilant masters at the FTC, this was a review copy that I received from the good folks at Wiley, who seem to like keeping me in Social Media, Job Search, and other business-oriented books!

As you no doubt have surmised, Ford R. Myers is a "career consultant" and Get The Job You Want Even When No One's Hiring[3] is his venture into systematizing a couple of decades' worth of experience into a generally-applicable book. His inspiration for this seems to be summed up in the following:

> We go through 12 years of education, possibly four more years of college, and sometimes even two to four more years of graduate school, and not one day is spent on how to manage your career, find work you truly enjoy, and make sure you're well compensated for it. Not one day!

One gets the idea that he decided to structure the book along the lines of how he might handle a new client, going from the current economic realities on through the various processes and on into a new job and beyond.

The book has an odd, albeit effective, structure, with 80-some numbered sections distributed over five "parts", plus a collection of "Career Resources" at the end. The sections vary substantially in length, with several being well under half a page, and others going on for many pages. One of the attractive things in this is the numerous examples of forms, letters, resume styles, check lists, etc. that he gives, all of which are available for download on his web site (http://www.CareerPotential.com/bookbonus), once you sign up for his mailing list.

While somewhat targeted to the mid-career executive who has found him- or herself out of work, Myers takes this from the beginning, with exercises that would be as applicable to a first-time job searcher as to a seasoned professional trying to find a new place in a less-than-optimal job market. In a dozen or so of these exercises the book walks you through figuring out what you ideally would like to be doing, how you'd like to be doing it, in what contexts/settings you'd like to be doing it, where that might be available, and coming up with transition strategies to get to that point.

Once this is determined, the focus shifts to developing "marketing" materials for one's search, from basics like the resume and cover letter, to suggestions for obtaining letters of recommendation, targeted networking (with various forms to track these contacts), and assorted extensions such as personal newsletters, web sites, and blogs. This is followed with sections on working with recruiters and others for getting to the right people at the right companies, advice for contacts and interviewing, and then into salary/benefit negotiations, the first 90 days on the job, and on-going career management strategies.

A very useful aspect here is the assorted "lists" of activities and action points to follow through a situation, be it across the job search in general, the "21 rules for negotiating", or the most helpful thing in the whole book (to me), a list of 42 suggested questions to ask when an interviewer opens the discussion up for your questions (I have occasionally found myself at a loss of anything appropriate to ask in those situations, and a review of this list prior to the interview would have come in very handy).

As noted, there is a lot here which I "have issues with", largely in terms of how the "generalized" advice applies to my particular case. However, for *most people* this is likely to be a very valuable walk-through of the job search process, and it is *certainly* going to save a lot of people the money they might have spent on a "career consultant" firm (and, trust me, 90% of what you'd be getting for the thousands of dollars those would cost are in this book, especially given the additional downloadable web resources connected with it).

Get The Job You Want[4] is relatively new, dating from last summer, and so should be available at your local brick-and-mortar book vendor, but Amazon has it at 1/3rd off (with their new/used guys not having it for much cheaper, a sign that its pretty popular). Despite the fact that reading this took me on a rollercoaster of reactions, from enthusiasm, to anger, to depression, etc., it certainly gets my recommendation as a very useful book for the job seeker (especially those who haven't been burned by the process repeatedly already).

Notes:

1. http://btripp-books.livejournal.com/93294.html
2. http://www.chicagonow.com/blogs/job-stalker/
3-4. http://amzn.to/1NPOnSV

Sunday, May 23, 2010[1]

If only ...

So, here's a "career" book that I actually *bought*, and "new" at that (which I'm noting due to so many recent books flowing through this space being either review copies from the publishers or things that I picked up via various sales)! I'd seen Timothy Ferriss' The 4-Hour Workweek: Escape 9-5, Live Anywhere, and Join the New Rich[2] cropping up on recommended reading lists for months, and figured I'd get a copy. This is the current "expanded and updated" version, which is nearly 100 pages longer than the first edition.

One thing that I need to say up front is that Timothy Ferriss has one of the most *amazing* resumes that I've ever seen, winning global contests in widely divergent activities he'd only had scant months of training in, and a relationship with academics that goes beyond "luck", so when he presents what seems to be the highly improbable as something to be achieved through a particular system, one has to consider that he might be on to something that the rest of us are not seeing. While this is enticingly presented in the early chapters of the book, you can also check out his web site (http://fourhourworkweek.com) for the broad strokes.

As one can gather from the title/subtitle, this is a book about getting out of the rat race and moving into a new sort of lifestyle. While many of the underlying drives expressed in this are, I think, common to most folks, there are elements which do make this a bit of a hard sell. Perhaps at the core of what's presented here is the classic story of the businessman vacationing in a fishing village who runs into a local fisherman who goes out to sea for a few hours in the morning, sells his catch, and spends the rest of the day loitering around the pub with his buddies, having a leisurely lunch with his wife, and spending a solid evening with his kids ... the visiting businessman asks why the fisherman doesn't "apply himself" to his trade, as it obviously could be much more lucrative than it is, to which the fisherman walks through all the points in the businessman's argument and points out that what the businessman is looking for in an eventual retirement scenario that the fisherman *already has* via his few hours of fishing! Ferriss suggests that there are ways to achieve similar freedoms in our life, given the right approach.

While there are *hundreds* of very useful resources, suggestions and directions in the book, I feel I should first raise some issues I had with it. The first is with his concept of one's "muse", which appears to be the "big idea" that one can come up with to escape the 9-to-5 with an independent (and hands-off out-sourced) business. When I spoke to him (for the interview in *The Job Stalker*[3] blog), I mentioned that I was somewhat unclear on the concept, and he insisted that it was all laid out in the "Finding the Muse" section. Well, I re-read this and still don't quite connect. Perhaps it's the choice of word, as, to me a "Muse" is something that would be deeply connecting and internal, and, frankly, the "Muse" of the book seems to be a *system* for trial-and-error attempts at businesses. While the *mechanics* of this process are pretty clearly laid out, the *ethos* of it seems missing ... except, of course, as a means to the end of achieving "Income Autopilot".

Reading these sections, I could never identify what this sort of thing could be *for me*, at least not in terms of something that I hadn't gone running after in the past and failed with. The examples here are, frankly, bordering on the bizarre for their extreme niche-orientation, from "French Navy sailor shirts" being marketed by one guy to "yoga for rock climbers" instructional videos being sold by another gal, to a very high-ticket collection of sound effect recordings being offered for video producers, etc. It is hard to imagine building a *sustainable* income off of these sorts of ventures.

This brings me to the other major qualm I had with the whole model here, the aim appears to be to live *like* the rich for periods of time ("mini-retirements" spread across one's working life), rather than actually *being* rich. Almost all the scenarios detailed here involve making a certain amount of money at home and then spending that on some foreign adventure over a number of months. Except for his own example (and Ferriss appears to be a serial entrepreneur), I found myself asking *"and then what?"* following stories of people spending months in South America, or whole seasons skiing in Europe. I, for one, am very fond of my home, and would be unwilling to part ways with it, but it seems that a lot of the "4-hour workweek philosophy" involves a very untethered existence which doesn't seem to spend a lot of time pumping up the kids' college funds.

Anyway, on the plus side, the book provides many ways of getting things done for cheap; the author uses several "virtual staffing" services out of India, which do pretty much everything for him in his various businesses (how he gets down to a 4-hour workweek, I guess), the examples given range from researching articles, preparing full presentations, to even one guy who (very temptingly) "outsourced" *his entire job search* successfully. Of course (speaking as somebody who has been struggling with long-term unemployment), if one is out of resources, and/or not in a fairly liquid cash flow situation, it is hard to see how one could make effective use of these services (and, I have come to understand, most of the resources listed in that area have become either much more expensive or significantly less reliable as they've dealt with the notoriety thrust on them by the book).

While I wouldn't say that the approach here is as "ethically challenged" as, for instance, I've seen in various affiliate marketing contexts on the web, there are certain fairly murky grey areas in this. For instance, to be an *"expert in the context of selling product means that you know more about the topic than the purchaser. No more. It is not necessary to be the best – just better than a small target number of your prospective customers."* ... this followed by a section purporting to teach you "How to Become a Top Expert in 4 Weeks". This, unfortunately, sounds to me like finding "the right suckers" to pitch your wares to.

Anyway, if the goals-in-context appeal to you (I have no *desire* for a 2-month ski vacation), and you're willing the be the sort of person to follow the business plans involved, there is a wealth of material in the book, both reproduced in its pages and downloadable from Ferriss' web site (which is a remarkable resource in its own right). The cost-per-experience breakdowns here would certainly help those so inclined to find enough people who would part with their money to make the reader's "dreamline" happen. Perhaps I'm just not the right "personality type" for this, while I (like most folks) would certainly welcome an "autopilot" income source, having it be both ethical and personally meaningful (as well as sustainable) would seem to be *requirements*, and, from my reading, that's not the focus here. Of course, if I were less "me", I might be a well-to-do lawyer or accountant or banker or politician (or "affiliate marketer"), rather than an out-of-work communications guy!

I really do hate to sound this negative about the book, as it was a fascinating read (and Mr. Ferriss very kindly made both an exception to his "no interviews" rule, and quite an effort to accommodate my requests) ... and there are many concepts in there which would be generally useful (from the term *eustress* to Pareto's 80/20 breakdown, and "Parkinson's Law", among numerous other gems) to anybody trying to build something for themselves. However, coming away from the book I found myself with little that I really wanted to try to implement (let alone the data junkie in me reacting to his advising of near-total disengagement from information flows!). While there is much of use in this book, I think it would take a particular sort of person to really make it work ... as much of this has almost a religious "cast off modern society and escape to a new way" evangelism to it.

The 4-Hour Workweek[4] is, of course, widely available, being a very popular title (it's #118 in Amazon's over-all books ratings, and #1 or #2 in a number of specific categories), so the odds of you being able to find it at your local brick-and-mortar bookstore are pretty good. As usual, however, Amazon has it at a substantial discount (43% off at this writing, which makes as cheap as any of the new/used guys' offerings), so that would be your best bet for getting a hold of this. Again, this was not a book that specifically spoke *to me*, but it certainly could be of great value to those chafing in their 9-5 jobs and looking for some way to escape to an envisioned retirement scenario (if in a series of work-retire-work-retire cycles in assorted dollar-value locales around the globe). As Dennis Miller would have it: *"Your mileage may vary!"* ... but it's worth checking out just in case it's the key you've been looking for.

Notes:

1. http://btripp-books.livejournal.com/93466.html

2. http://amzn.to/1QmMvlv

3. http://www.chicagonow.com/job-stalker/2010/05/maybe-something-thats-not-a-job/

4. http://amzn.to/1QmMvlv

Saturday, May 29, 2010[1]

Good advice, no nagging

Ever since I started doing reviews of job/career/business books over in *The Job Stalker*[2] blog and began contacting publishers' PR folks to set up mini e-mail interviews with various authors, I've begun to see more and more books being sent out to me for review. This is the first of two books provided to me by Ten Speed Press (hellllooo, FTC) recently. Since I'd been giving myself a bit of a break from the "heavy duty" industry books (well, that's not quite true, I'm about half way through a book on technological innovations intended for a "C-Level" audience), I figured that I'd slip these in just to have something to feature over on that blog!

Casey Hawley's 10 Make-or-Break Career Moments: Navigate, Negotiate, and Communicate for Success[3] takes an interesting approach to career advice, no doubt originating, to a certain extent, from her sitting "on the other side of the table" (most of her previous books being guides for *management* rather than individual employees). She's listed as a "Communications Consultant" and that's certainly where this book is coming from, offering communications coaching for 10 key challenges or turning points within one's professional life.

Frankly, I had a rather odd "strongest take-away" from this book, and that is more in an experiential than informational mode: the tone is *remarkably* neutral. As I've noted in previous reviews, I have certain "issues" with career coaches and other similar job-advice-giving folks ... yet I was about 1/3rd through reading this when I realized that I did *not* feel like I was being *lectured to* by some self-appointed "expert" (which is frequently a point of irritation in other "career advice" books). Instead the book read more like an in-depth study by an outside observer who was trying to present as unbiased an assessment of the subject matter as possible. This was, to me, "a breath of fresh air" in a genre that typically reads with a subtext of *"because I say so!"*.

If there was one thing I'd change/add here it would be a collection of key points in the back. The author is somewhat fond of creating memory-jogging acronyms (or as she calls them, "models") for various situations, from M.I.S.S.I.O.N. to B.E.A.C.O.N., B.L.U.R., and D.U.C.K., and these would be simply referred to in chapters after those in which they were defined. I found these somewhat confusing, and wished there was a back-of-the-book page with these broken down into their component elements, as well as some notations on other concepts. Admittedly, it's a minor point, but it would have made the information flow of the book far clearer.

What *are* the "10 Make-or-Break Career Moments"? They span much of an individual's career arc: "the first moment you meet an executive or other key business contact", "the first moment you meet the interviewer for your next job", "the moment you are offered a job", "the key moment in a performance review", "the moment you meet your new team", "the moment you are fired", "the moment a challenge to your ethics, loyalty, or future arises", "the moment you resign from a job", "the moment conflict arises with a coworker or other businessperson", and "the moment you are recognized for excellence". In addition, there is a concluding section where the author profiles a half a dozen notable executives, and showing how *they* used techniques similar to those outlined in the text.

Each of these "career moments" gets its own chapter, with various levels of advice, from the "philosophical" to the specifically practical, ranging (naturally enough) from the very basic (in the introductory chapters) to the more advanced as the book moves into issues of more senior positions ... in all cases the material is direct, clear, and (perhaps most refreshingly) "not preachy". I certainly enjoyed reading this more that I had anticipated I would, and found good information for my own use.

10 Make-or-Break Career Moments[4] is, of course, brand new, so should be out in your local brick-and-mortar book store. It has a very reasonable cover price, and Amazon currently has it at a decent discount ... oddly enough, there are already copies in the new/used channel, and a "like new" copy can be had through that for under five bucks. Again, if you're looking for a bit of coaching for your business communications, this would be a solid place to start, with good advice an "no attitude", putting it far ahead of much of its category!

Notes:

1. http://btripp-books.livejournal.com/93913.html
2. http://www.chicagonow.com/blogs/job-stalker/
3-4. http://amzn.to/233TWEe

Sunday, May 30, 2010[1]

Touring history ...

I don't usually "bunch up" books (although I have, with some very short books in a series, done so before) but when I was contemplating what I was going to write about the three *Traveler's Guide to the Ancient World* books that I just got done with, I realized that much of what I was going to be saying was either going to be substantially the same for each of these, unless I did some serious tap-dancing in the attempt to say the same thing without saying the same thing. I took a look out on the web to see if there were *more* in this series, and it appears that these three are it, and that their original publisher (Quid, from the UK) has since come out with a combined edition (making me feel more justified in taking these on as a group). These are the US editions (from Metro Books, if you care), which I picked up in the after-after-after-holiday sale by B&N (part of the 13 books I got for two bucks a piece).

These books are structured to resemble popular travel series such as Fodor's, Frommers or Lonely Planet, under the name *Traveler's Guide to the Ancient World*. Each deals with a notable location, at a particular point in time. The three books here, dealing with Rome, Athens, and Thebes, are logical enough for their locations (although one would like to imagine what *other* books in the series might have ended up covering), but it must have been an interesting discussion as to *when* the books would be featuring these cities and their environs.

Each of these is remarkably similar, with the same lay-out, design, flow, and even page count, with the same artists providing illustrations, etc. One might expect that these would have also all been written by the same person, but that's not the case, each featuring (what one assumes to be) an expert on that place and time to provide the vivifying details of the living city in that particular era (as a former publisher it makes me wonder if the concept came before the development, or if there were some vaguely similar manuscripts sitting around that were then focused into the "travel guide" concept!).

Following an introduction that sort of gives "the lay of the land" (culturally, geographically, and historically) each book is in six sections, 1 – A Concise Background, 2 - The City of XXX, 3 – Surrounding Areas, 4 – Entertaining on a Budget, 5 – Practical Considerations, and 6 – References and Resources. The editing is tight enough that in every book the start of the second part, Section 4, starts on page 100, while the Index appears on page 158 (each being just 160 pages long). The books cover various aspects of the history, culture, social order, modes of travel, housing, food, shopping, entertainment, and various daily need-to-know data such as weights, measures, and currency. I opted to read these in chronologically reverse order, going from the most recent to the most ancient.

The first of these, then, is Traveler's Guide to The Ancient World – The Roman Empire: Rome and its Environs in the Year 300 CE[2], written by Dr. Ray Laurence. Now, I am reasonably conversant on Roman history, but it was interesting to have this "window" onto Rome be in a more transitional period, that of dual, but connected, Emperors, each bearing the title of "Augustus", Diocletian and Maximian, and each having a chosen (but non-hereditary) successor bearing the title of "Caesar". At this time, Rome ruled the whole of the Mediterranean, from the Nile Valley to Gibraltar and from Hadrian's Wall, western Europe with borders along the Rhine and Danube, and nearly to Babylon. What is fascinating here, of course, is reading what is new, and what is already old in the period, many brand-new features of the city being discussed have long disappeared in our age, but others (already old in the time-line of the book) can still be seen. Obviously, of these three, Rome is the most familiar, as by 300 CE much of what we would recognize as "modern urban life" was in place, from a standardized currency, a broad product-based economy, and even traffic snarls.

Next came Traveler's Guide to The Ancient World – Ancient Greece: Athens and its Environs in the Year 415 BCE[3], written by Eric Chaline. This runs the clock back another 700 years, and looks at Athens in a period of reconstruction, a couple of generations past the destruction of the city by the Persians, and only 16 years since the start of the Peloponnesian War (and long struggle with Sparta). At this time, the Greeks (the Athenians and others) are just one element in the Mediterranean political spectrum, and of much smaller extent than either the Carthaginians or the Persians. Obviously, modern democracies owe their philosophical foundations to Athens, and it is fascinating to see the forms in which Athenian democracy expresses itself. It is also very interesting to take a look at the polytheistic system which was core to the cultural sensibilities of the day, and how that intertwined with the philosophical and political aspects of the civilization. Notably, the military struggles of the time cast shadows here, with warnings about travel, and what to be on the watch for in the area around Athens.

Finally, there's Traveler's Guide to The Ancient World – Ancient Egypt: Thebes and the Nile Valley in the Year 1200 BCE[4], written by Charlotte Booth. This takes us to possibly the greatest period of Egyptian power, in the waning days of Ramses The Great's reign. In the time-frame of the book, Ramses had been on the throne for an amazing *sixty-five years*, and nearly all of his mortuary temples, etc. had been completed decades earlier (indeed, one of the reasons he is so well remembered is that his workmen had *generations* to work on things like the Ramesseum, which took more than 20 years to create ... unlike later kings whose far briefer reigns demanded far less grandiose constructions). At this point Egypt was already ancient, with ruins and monuments that were 1500 years old by the time, and because of this, this is more like a "travel book" than the others in the series, as there are many "tourist spots" to cover! Culturally, one of the most notable things is the lack of currency, and the visitor is advised as to what would be best to bring for trade ... which creates a very alien sense of commerce to the modern mind.

Obviously, there's a conceit to these, that puts them in an odd middle zone between historical fiction and quasi-archaeological exposition, as the reader *knows* that these are not "travel books" for real, but is asked to "suspend disbelief" sufficiently to absorb the "feel" of these times and locales. On the plus side, these do focus a lot more light on the daily details of life in these cultures that one would be likely to find in most other books (an example: all three of them give instructions for procuring and paying *for prostitutes*, aside from the more "expected" niceties of travel!), which certainly leaves even the history enthusiast more informed about these places than they would likely to have been previously.

These are currently out of print, but both Amazon and B&N show them as available via the new/used vendors (at various price points), however the individual editions (and the combined 3-in-1 edition) seem to still be available from their original publisher in the UK, Quid[5], which might work out better (even with international shipping) should you want to check these out!

Notes:

1. http://btripp-books.livejournal.com/94156.html
2. http://amzn.to/1SMWK9x
3. http://amzn.to/24hUPM1
4. http://amzn.to/1QyKmlD
5. http://www.quidpublishing.com/

Sunday, June 6, 2010[1]

A beginner's manual for the business world ...

A month or so back, I was surprised to receive a package containing review copies of couple of "job search" book from Ten Speed Press (oooh, call the FTC ... they're sending him *free books!*). I was somewhat surprised by this, as I'd previously either been *queried* as to my interest in reviewing new titles, or had to reach out to the publishers myself on books I thought would be good to cover in my The Job Stalker[2] blog over on the Chicago Tribune's "Chicago Now" blogging site. As I noted last week, these ended up being a pleasant surprise (having much more in them of value to me than I had anticipated at first glance), and were *certainly* on-target for the blog.

Needless to say, the odds of my "free range" picking up Effective Immediately: How to Fit In, Stand Out, and Move Up at Your First Real Job[3] by Emily Bennington and Skip Lineberg would have been rather low, given this being sub-titularly targeted for those going into their "first REAL JOB". I had even joked to the PR rep at the publisher who'd sent these that it was going to feel funny reading this on the El and buses (where I get most of my reading done), with having folks checking out the cover, and then wondering what a grey-beard like me was doing reading *that*! So, I was very pleased to find what an informative and witty read this ended up being. One of the "best things" about this is that it is broken up into about 100 quarter-page to 9-page "chapters" (along with assorted "newbie to newbie" features where now-successful professionals warn the reader about career mis-steps they'd made in their younger years), spread out across five "Parts" which take the reader from the first day in a "real job" on through becoming a leader and a mentor. This format ensures that the authors never stay "too long" on a point, while going long when necessary (there are several sections here which are *brilliant* condensations of what's involved in writing articles, creating work plans, making budgets, conducting project management, etc.).

This brings me to my main take-away from the book: while I'm *sure* this would be super for the newly-hired kid fresh out of school, it is also *extremely* useful for anybody out there who's a "school of hard knocks" professional, who, while broadly educated (like yours truly), never took a "business class" in their life, yet had spent a whole career doing many of these basic business functions "by the seat of their pants". In the middle section where many of these were covered, I found myself thinking *"Gee, wish I'd had this when I started my publishing company!"* ... although I realize that it's a wholly different "franchise", but this book reads more like a "Basic Business for Dummies" than a book *exclusively* for new workers.

Again, the staccato-fire format here is handy as it allows for a lot variation in the material, a section about what to wear to work (and *why*) can be quickly followed with "coaching" about how one's arrival in the office mix is likely to be largely ignored (except for being subjected to "brain dumps" of details), a list of key business books (to both be read *and* left out where they can be noticed at your desk) to obtain, organizations one should join, etc. Not to get into cross-generational "attention" sniping, this certainly allows the authors to "build up a picture" of what the new hire can expect without going into 50-page dissertations on "what you can expect on your first day at work". Also valuable are the little "psychological" points dropped in here which help defuse the stress one might expect to feel around assorted meetings, etc., and look at what your boss and other associates *want* out of various exchanges, and how best address those factors rather than simply the surface-level structures.

Needless to say, I found Bennington & Lineberg's Effective Immediately[4] a remarkably refreshing and (for somebody with 30 years of business experience) *useful* read. I really hope this finds a wider audience than *just* the starting worker (although this would make a very nice graduation gift!), as the material it presents is likely to be beneficial to everybody other than know-it-all MBAs (who you can't tell anything to anyway). Being a brand new release, this is no doubt available via your local bookstore, although Amazon has it for about 1/3rd off the already very reasonable cover price, making that option even cheaper than the used vendors, with shipping. Again, while this is very much an ideal book for its targeted audience, many others out there will find it both an entertaining and helpful read.

Notes:

1. http://btripp-books.livejournal.com/94416.html
2. http://www.chicagonow.com/blogs/job-stalker/
3-4. http://amzn.to/1rv8G3G

Thursday, June 10, 2010[1]

Great info ... for corporate execs

Occasionally I read a book because I figure "it will do me good" ... sometimes these are classics that somehow fell through the cracks in my education, sometimes they're things that "might be useful" in a career setting. This is one of the latter sort. Frankly, this came to me sort of out-of-the-blue from Wiley (alert to FTC nanny-state over-lords: this was a review copy provided to me without charge) and it really didn't "fit" with most of my reading. However, when looking it over, it seemed like it might be one of those books that I'd be better for having read, so I plowed into it.

Phil Simon's The Next Wave of Technologies: Opportunities in Chaos[2] is not what one would call a "fun" book, and it's not even a "gripping" book, but I suppose it does come in as a "useful" book as it provides current snap-shots of more than a dozen "technologies" which are likely to effect business over the next several years. The nominal author, Phil Simon, did pen parts of this, but it appears that his primary function was pulling together a team of subject experts who would each address one of the topical areas. As he notes in the introductory material, there was no way that one writer could amass sufficient knowledge across all these subjects in enough time to write an up-to-date book on them, so he assembled a group of writers who had published on each, and then edited the results into a reasonably single-toned whole.

This book also has a fairly narrowly-targeted audience:

> I started thinking about the need for a book that would address the essentials, best practices, and pitfalls of these exciting new technologies. Wouldn't a book like this be beneficial to C-level executives unsure about what to do and how to do it? A busy chief information office (CIO) could read this book and walk away with a much deeper, practical understanding of these new concepts. The same CIO might walk into work the next day and ask "Why aren't we doing this?"

Yes, this is pretty much targeted towards the upper management of corporations, which each section involving a "what this is", "how this works", "how to implement it" structure. Needless to say, the "casual reader" (myself included) is likely left a bit in the dust of concerns focused on the C-Suites.

Also, the quote above illustrates one of my main peeves with this book, most terms get spelled out with their acronym *once*, and if that particular usage didn't quite sink in while reading past it, a lot of sections read more like a football huddle call than a lucid discussion. Yes, if one flipped back to the Index you could find out what a particular set of letters *meant*, but there are *dozens* of these throughout the book, and their systematic usage (frequently saving a fairly minimal number of characters over actually spelling out what was being discussed!) was, to me at least, an on-going source of irritation.

Anyway, here's what's covered in The Next Wave of Technologies[3]: Cloud Computing, Open Source, Software as Service, Service-Oriented Architecture, Managing Mobile Business, Social Networking, Enterprise Search and Retrieval, Enterprise 2.0 Business Intelligence, Master Data Management, Procure-to-Pay, Agile Software Development, Enterprise Risk Management, Global Engineering, plus sections on Project Failure, Sustainability and "Green" business, implementing projects within an organization, etc. I must admit, that with one or two exceptions, none of these were things I had a burning desire to know about, but at least now, were I to find myself in a conversation which was inexplicably floating off towards "Enterprise Risk Management", I'll now be able to muster more than an incredulous blank stare.

Obviously, this is *not* a book for everyone, but if you're in its target audience, I'm sure you will find this an informative and wide-ranging look at subjects in which you, too, might not have a solid background. Another factor making this an "elite" book is its rather remarkably high cover price … sixty bucks! I guess "corporate library" books get the same sort of mark-up that textbooks usually come with. Fortunately, "the magic of the marketplace" is already in play here, with Amazon having it at a 37% discount (for a still-hefty $37.80) and their new/used vendors having this "new" for as little as just over twenty dollars. I suppose if one is CIO of Pretty Big Corp. Inc., shelling out the cover price wouldn't be an issue, but for the rest of us who might find this sort of an overview *useful*, it's nice to know there are alternatives!

Again, this is hardly a book for "everybody", but it's a quality study of the current state of a wide array of technologies and technologically-oriented trends within the context of how they'd impact business. If one is within those fairly tightly-set crosshairs, this would certainly be a recommended read, but for the rest of the population, it's probably not stuff about which you have any particular need to know.

Notes:

1. http://btripp-books.livejournal.com/94574.html

2-3. http://amzn.to/1YQFNcw

Friday, June 11, 2010[1]

An oldie but goodie ...

OK, so I'm pretty much embarrassed that it's taken me this long to get around to reading any of Seth Godin's books, at least in context of my recent "expertise" in books of this sort as reflected in my scribblings on The Job Stalker[2] blog. I would remind the too-quick-to-chide reader that I had pretty much avoided all "business books" until just the past year, and will use that excuse to justify my coming to this party late.

Unlike many of the books I've written about here in this particular genre, this did not come to me as a review copy, but was ordered used from Amazon, due to having heard it referenced over and over again in other sources. Seth Godin's Permission Marketing: Turning Strangers Into Friends And Friends Into Customers[3] is a classic, and is remarkably fresh for being over a decade old. The vast majority of the book would still be cutting-edge today despite its rather hoary vintage (within the Social Media genre), which really indicates just how visionary it was when published. To get a sense of just how old this book is, I present this quote:

> Never build anything that isn't fun on a 14.4 modem

... that was, of course, 14.4 kilobits/second, not the 14.4 megabits/second of a good 3G connection on a smartphone! So, obviously, Godin didn't have a crystal ball (he was also predicting the immanent demise of banner ads on the web thanks to those new-fangled "cookie" things that had just been introduced).

Over-all, however, the message here of personal interaction with the customer is as solid now as it was then, and has, to a great extent, only been really implemented by the most savvy of the better marketers, with the grey-force drone army of MBAs still marching to the tried-and-true (as noted here: "nobody every got fired for running an ad") rather than the better and brighter. As clear a case as Godin lays out here, it is remarkable how rare (and notable) the well-implemented Permission Marketing program is ten years down the line.

Frankly, having been immersed in Web 2.0, Social Media, and assorted cutting-edge web marketing technologies over the past 3 years, this book has a certain bizarre edge to it. It is, if anything, as up-to-date in its calls to action as anything that I've read in my recent spate of books of this type. However, so much of it (like the modem comment above) is incredibly dated, with companies he's trumpeting as "doing it right" being long-lost victims to other trends, and others he takes to task, chugging along with the same-old-same-old quite profitably still.

I would, however, heartily recommend Permission Marketing[4] to all and sundry (OK, to all those with an interest in marketing and modern Internet culture), as it is such a clear-eyed look at how much better so much could be if we just weaned ourselves away from old habits. One of the more fascinating things in here is a general timeline he sketches out of how we got to the "advertising model", from a century or so ago when most stuff we used around the house was hand (or even home) made, and not mass produced, to the evolution of mass production, "products" (the story of Crisco is particularly fascinating), and branding, and how advertising related to this all.

As noted, I got this via the Amazon new/used guys for a substantial discount (I ordered a "good" copy of the hardcover which I was very pleased to find was closer to "like new"), but it is still in print should you want to run out and pick up a copy at your local brick-and-mortar book vendor (and Amazon has it at a 34% discount). It's a classic, and some of the specifics are certainly dated, but the message of the book (and most of the techniques) is as solid as when it first came out, and this is certainly something that every web marketer/developer should have at hand.

Notes:

1. http://btripp-books.livejournal.com/94844.html
2. http://www.chicagonow.com/blogs/job-stalker/
3-4. http://amzn.to/1Qxt2O3

Tuesday, June 15, 2010[1]

Dollar store dreams ...

Here's another dollar store find. Every week when my daughters have their martial arts classes, I make an effort to run over to the dollar store up by their Dojo to check out what's new. I have been amazed at what I've found there over the years, and I'm certainly always *thrilled* to get an engaging, informative, or amusing volume at 96% (or thereabouts) off of cover price! The selection is never *fabulous*, but it is always in flux, so while there not might be anything of interest (and, again, I'm somewhat limited in what appeals to me, as I pretty much only read non-fiction these days) for weeks at a time, some days I walk out of there with five or six books.

Of course, the dynamic of the dollar store book channel generally leads to a *"oh, that sounds interesting"* selection criteria, as one rarely runs across titles that were on one's "wishlist". I had never heard of William T. Vollmann, despite his having written a dozen or so books, but his Riding Toward Everywhere[2] was sitting there, and looked like an interesting memoir, and so I picked it up.

I suppose that had I known more of Vollmann, I would have been in a better state for plowing into this ... I have since discovered that many of his titles (based in various places around the world, he is certainly an "adventurous" author) are presented as "dreams", and that is very much the feel here. Although certainly in "memoir" territory, this telling lacks much of the place/time context cues that one would typically expect, rather being a rambling digression on the author's hobby of riding freight trains. I say "hobby" as he evidently has no *need* of "riding the rails" as a latter-day hobo, he and his (equally middle-class) traveling companions fly, bus, and even pay for their train transport on their ways to and from their freight adventures, so this seems to be some "mash-up" of one man's model railroad and another's RV'ing, bringing some sort of enrichment into their lives.

Part of the attraction appears to be in the *literary* heritage of the "traveling life", as he frequently quotes Jack London, Kerouac, Hemingway, Twain, Thomas Wolfe, and others whose experiences Vollmann appears to be trying to, in some degree, recapture. Although, again, this is no linear narrative, no history of his experiences, just a tumble of images from the rails, and the environment of those who still ride them. The thought occurred to me at a couple of points, that Riding Toward Everywhere[3] was almost more of a *poem* (although without any pretense of formal structuring) than other form, unless of course, this is what constitutes the "dreams" of his several titles that bear that designation. Here's one passage where this was particularly notable:

> *I wandered the hot and narrow brick alley-canyons, my gaze defeated by gratings; then came windows all nacreous like husks of sea-things, every pane different, and there was the smell of garbage. Was this all there was to being anywhere? In the alley where someone had written on the brickwork I HATE MY LIFE, there came a view of the elevated tracks, and upon them a string of dark brownish-grey BNSF gainer cars. The cars did not move.*

Another notable thing of this book is that it is about two thirds text and one third photos, although not set out to *illustrate* the text as one might expect. Despite the fact that people and places from the book appear in the pictures (and so certainly *could* have been interspersed with the copy), they all come in a block at the end, with a brief identifying section (with what would have been "captions" had they actually appeared with the images). Why is it like this? Who knows, perhaps to further the nonlinear aspects, as recognizing the images from the descriptions well after the reading part is done. All in all, this is an intriguing book, and the caveats of the author's purpose for being there are only a slightly distracting undercurrent (for me, at least ... I was on some levels wanting to know more about his life when he "went back to his real world" to put this into some sort of context beyond the bits dropped of foreign travel or family concerns). If it is a "dream" of riding the rails, it's an enjoyable one to indulge in for a time.

How *does* a book like Riding Toward Everywhere[4] (first edition hardcover) end up at the dollar store? Well, my first thought is that, like several other "finds" covered here, this falls between standard categories, and might not have "found its audience" and so gone out of print. However, this might not be the case on this, as it's available in a slightly later paperback edition, and Amazon still has copies of the hardcover at full price (although "like new" used copies are in their system for as little as 27¢, plus shipping). So, maybe (as has appeared to have been the case previously), I was "just lucky" to hit a dump of *that* book in *that* dollar store on *that* day. This certainly is a hard call as far as a recommendation goes, however, being firmly in the "your mileage may vary" territory. If a dream-like portrait of a middle-aged, middle-class man indulging in his passion "for the rails" in a current time frame sounds like it would appeal to you, by all means, seek this out, but I imagine that this isn't the sort of thing that would appeal to all-and-sundry, although I found it a pleasant enough read.

Notes:

1. http://btripp-books.livejournal.com/95020.html

2-4. http://amzn.to/231D29u

Sunday, June 20, 2010[1]

I Tweet therefore I am ...

I had Shel Israel's Twitterville: How Businesses Can Thrive in the New Global Neighborhoods[2] on my "to read" list since hearing him speak at the Social Media Club of Chicago's meeting last fall. As regular readers know, I'm an avid Twitterer, and have been "following" Shel (@ShelIsrael) since that presentation. I did, however, wait to pick up a copy of his book until it had come down to my "price point" via the Amazon new/used vendors (sorry Shel!), at which point I snapped up a copy.

Twitterville[3] is an odd sort of book, one that's somewhat between genres. Israel's background is in journalism, and on one level, this reads like the stories of a "beat writer" assigned to the virtual locale of *Twitterville* ... these are the stories of the 140-character city, that Twitterin' Town. It starts with an American imprisoned in Egypt, whose furtive tweets to home unleashed a viral tide that managed to get usually slow-to-turn wheels of government to spin into actions that had him soon freed. This was the event that grabbed Shel's attention to the world of Twitter, and focused his attentions on its neighborhoods.

I have been involved in Twitter for several years, from my previous position as the Communications Director of a "metaverse developer" working primarily in the virtual world of Second Life ... I had discovered there that much of the business of Second Life was *not* being conducted "in world", but via Twitter by the likes of tech investor Mitch Kapor (@mkapor). I found that by following him, and those he followed, and the folks following him, I was getting massive amounts of "business intelligence" for the mere cost of my attention.

This is widely divergent to the attitude that many people have about Twitter ... that this is the place where people who would typically be driving their friends nuts with texts about what they were having for lunch, or how crowded the mall was, etc., were now spewing their inanity for the whole world's consumption. Israel has a very telling description of this misconception early on in the book:

> This {the live-blogging of South-by-Southwest conference programs evolving into live-Tweeting "collaborative journalism"} also became evidence to refute the conventional but misguided perception that Twitter was just another example of gabby kids' stuff. Adult professionals addressing a business problem had started Twitter. Its early adopters and proponents may have been young, but they were business professionals. This was an early – and important – differentiation from Facebook and MySpace, whose respective user bases were college and high school students.

This is the appeal of Twitter, a way to reach out to a whole world of opinion leaders and influential minds who might not have been accessible any other way. Much of what is covered in the book is the almost accidental discovery of the platform by various companies, and how it has been used and misused in various contexts by various groups.

Make no mistake, there are still fairly high-profile companies which barely register on the Twitter screen at all, while there are others who feel like they "live there". In some cases, this simply evolved from a few key employees finding and using the channel, which then slowly spread through the organization and came to be accepted as a valuable tool. In others a top-down approach was tried where upper management requested a "Twitter strategy" and some versions worked and some didn't. There have been many cases where the dynamics of Twitter certainly clashed with corporate dictates (such as Nestle's recent gaffe where one of their Twitter reps was threatening users sporting Nestle-oriented user icons with actions on trademark violations). One of the concepts that the author floats here is of "lethal generosity", *"a phenomenon used by the smartest companies ... in social media the greatest influence invariably goes to the most generous participants, not the loudest"* where if you give more to the on-line community than your competition, *"the other player is forced either to follow you or to abstain from participating"*.

If there was one thing I'd like to see different about this book it would be achieving a better balance between the broad social impact (such as the lead story with the arrest in Egypt, as well as the Twitter element in various global events), and the "business angle". The narrative here keeps dipping a toe into a more "general" stream, but keeps finding its way back to the Business story. Sure, this is what gets focused on in the book's sub-title, but (as a user) this makes it feel like it's being limited. Going in to this, the reader should be very clear on the fact that they're reading a book about *business* operating within "Twitterville", and not a broader survey of that world … almost like coming in to a new town and picking up a local paper and discovering, aside from a few highlights on the front page, there was *only* the Business section to be had. So, while this will (as detailed above) help to dissuade folks who lump Twitter in with other Social Media outlets, it is also not an "introductory book" to get people interested (outside of a business context, of course) in Twitter (while a "Getting Started" section *is* included, it's relegated to a 4-page Afterword).

<u>Twitterville</u>[4] certainly is recommended to anybody with an interest in the business use of Social Media. Being fairly new (it just came out last Fall), it should be available at your local brick-and-mortar book vendor who has a business and/or internet section. Amazon currently has it almost half-priced, and the new/used guys currently have "like new" copies for under a couple of bucks (plus shipping, of course). Admittedly I'm biased, as I'm a long-term resident of "Twitterville", but I hope a lot of people read this book, as I get tired of having to explain how Twitter is "serious business" and not just "chatting with (virtual) friends"!

Notes:
1. http://btripp-books.livejournal.com/95428.html
2-4. http://amzn.to/1YQEudH

Monday, June 28, 2010[1]

Retro reading ...

Sometimes I'll take the advice of one author to go check out books by another author without doing much research on them. In this case, when I interviewed Timothy Ferriss over in The Job Stalker[2] blog, one of the "other resources" he recommended was David J. Schwartz's The Magic of Thinking Big[3], and I surfed over to Amazon to pick up a used copy. How odd.

Considering how *outré* Mr. Ferriss' systems are, and how deeply entangled with state-of-the-art technologies, it is almost *bizarre* that he was recommending this book. This was written in the 1950's and, while updated in the mid-60's, has the feel of coming from a *Leave it to Beaver* world, perhaps crossed with *The Dick Van Dyke Show* in its update. Dr. Schwartz was a college professor (I've not been able to determine in what field he had a doctorate) and the head of a consulting firm specializing in "leadership development". It was in this role that he encountered many men coming out of the service (World War II experiences are frequently referred to in discussing individuals here), who sought out his advice for their peace-time careers.

Of course, having a "vintage feel" does not necessarily mean that a book has moved beyond its usefulness, after all, Napoleon Hill's *Think and Grow Rich* was penned in the last Great Depression and is still motivating people today, however The Magic of Thinking Big[4] also comes from a period of unequaled economic expansion, and much of what Dr. Schwartz writes in here sounds extremely pollyannaish in the current economy, especially as it relates to jobs. It seems that any of the people he talked to were able to find a job, even in a new field, in a matter of *weeks*, and that "opportunities" were there for the taking. Speaking as somebody who has been in the job search in present conditions for well over a *year*, this quickly leads one to have doubts about how useful the advice is to the modern reader.

Other elements are "stuck in time" here as well. This book was written in a period without global trade as we know it now. Do you recall the days when "Made in Japan" indicated a product was a cheap, poorly-constructed alternative to something domestic? I do, but just barely (and I'm just a year or two older than this book). Schwartz makes a point of encouraging readers to buy *the most expensive* shirts, suits, shoes, etc. on the *assumption* that they're going to be better and last longer ... contrast this to the world today when price is largely a function of brand-name and marketing, and the *cheapest* item available might very well be produced side-by-side with the most expensive one in some factory in China, with one getting the "name" identification and the other (virtually identical item) going out "generic". Similar "dated" conceptions are through the book, with assumptions that many of the men trying to find their place in the post-war economy were coming from rural or similarly "not up to speed" locations, and coaching them how to "fit in". Hardly a factor in the "mono-culture" that TV and its mass communications successors have created in the US, if not the world.

All this being said, there are some very good bits of advice in here, still worthwhile once the matrix of the '50s and '60s is scraped off. Material about the attributes of leaders, how not to sabotage your own efforts, how to properly take risks and make plans, all are applicable in today's world. Unfortunately, so much of this is tied into stories of individuals that it's like trying to extract life lessons from 1950's sitcoms, possible, but needing a whole lot of filtering!

I must admit, there was an added veneer of cynicism for me here, as the used copy that I'd bought had been previously owned by a rather eager highlighter whose mark-up of the book tells a story all its own. I'm assuming that this person got this via some self-help seminar and was totally gung-ho to plow into this, as many paragraphs are underlined, exclamation marks added in the margins, asterisks pointing out sections, lists items circled, etc. ... right up to the half-way point in the book, where they stop. Of course, being the cynic that I am, I spun all sorts of scenarios explaining this, but I found the exuberance irritating while it lasted!

The Magic of Thinking Big[5] is still in print, so if you feel like getting your "secrets of success" wrapped up in retro packaging, you will certainly be able to find a copy. It's fairly inexpensive, and Amazon has it discounted to just over ten bucks, but a "good" used copy can be had for under a quarter (plus S&H, of course). Personally, I'd like to see a "modern" version of this, perhaps a condensation of the "timeless" parts ... between experiencing bitterness over the comparable economies, and the snarkiness over the previous owner's evidently time-limited enthusiasm, I really didn't much enjoy reading this, and probably "got" less of the messages that have kept this in print for half a century that I would have otherwise. Definitely a "your mileage may vary" case ... not something I'd particularly recommend, but not a total waste either.

Notes:

1. http://btripp-books.livejournal.com/95647.html

2. http://bit.ly/9M3hMO

3-5. http://amzn.to/1QxrJi6

Monday, July 5, 2010[1]

Science!

Sometimes I'm surprised by a book, but this book *came to me* somewhat as a surprise. I'd been kvetching a bit with one of the PR gals from Wiley about how I "couldn't wait to get a job so I could quit *reading* job search books", and indicated that some of the stuff I'd otherwise be reading included popular physics books. I guess she made a note of this, as when the next "business" book review copy showed up, there was *also* a copy of Paul Halpern's Collider: The Search for the World's Smallest Particles[2], which made me feel all warm and fuzzy inside (since, obviously, there wasn't much chance of my reviewing this over in The Job Stalker[3]).

The *other* main surprise about this book is that it is only *thematically* about the LHC (Large Hadron Collider) at CERN. I had wondered when this came in how one might have cranked out a whole book about the LHC when it had only very recently been put back (after a bit of a melt-down when it was first fired up) on-line. Instead, this is a rather exquisite history of sub-atomic particle physics, within the context of the development and goals of the LHC program. I understand that some others have found this a *weakness* in the book (looking, I must assume, for an in-depth over-view of the LHC), but I was very pleased to find this the thrust of the book.

The book begins with the LHC in a Prologue and then moves to something of a "thumbnail" of the history of the science and politics which led to the LCH in the Introduction. At this point, however, it abandons the present and runs the clock all the way back to the ancient philosophic antecedents of "atomic theory", and the 16th-18th century scientists who sought ways of understanding matter and energy. These philosophic/scientific aspects fill the first few chapters, rolling through the years up to Einstein, and into the Theoretical struggles (attempts at a Theory of Everything, and various related permutations, string theory, supersymmetry, Higgs fields, multiverses, etc.) of the current era. Once all this is established, Halpern turns to the meat of the book, looking at how we got from there to here in the context of the laboratory.

One of the more engaging aspects of the telling is the inclusion of a good amount of biographical detail about the main figures. While I have read quite a deal on the *science*, I don't believe I've ever picked up a biography of any of the *scientists* (well, I guess with the exception of Feynman's autobiographical books), and it was fascinating to see where the "leading lights" of this area of physics had come from.

The story picks up with Ernest Rutherford, and is thick with names, familiar and new (to me), and their theories, experiments, collaborations, and conflicts. One chapter covers the late 1800's through the early 1920's, with all the amazing expansion that physics made then. Next is turns to the development of the accelerators, looking at the early research, and early advocates, while focusing on the career of Ernest Lawrence. From here it shifts back to theory, looking at forces and how they interact with various particles; this involving Fermi, Gamow, and QED (Quantum ElectroDynamics), along with a raft of other Big Names.

At this point the big colliders come to the fore, in a chapter (largely led by Robert R. Wilson, a protégé of Lawrence who created Fermilab and the Tevatron, and Carlo Rubbia, who spurred on CERN) that looks at the development of the main American and European facilities. This walks the reader through the search for ever-higher energies, and the scientific challenges towards finding ways of experimentally validating the predictions of QCD (Quantum ChromoDynamics, which deals with the sub-sub-atomic world of quarks, etc.), and runs pretty much up to the mid-1980's (with a bit of a forward jump to the 1995 announcement by two teams at Fermilab of the discovery of the top quark).

The next section covers the sad tale of the Superconducting Super Collider – the mammoth (the collider was to have a 54-mile circumference ring!) device begun under Reagan, but canceled under Clinton. This part deals more with politics and the issues of funding such huge projects, but also considers the science involved and the fallout (and continuing effects) on atomic physics in the U.S. from the program's cancellation. Here the book turns to CERN, and looks at the development of the LHC, noting the differences of how "big science" is funded in the European context, but also going into quite a lot of detail in what is involved in that machine.

Again, the book shifts focus, now back to theory, and looks at dark matter, dark energy, and the current thought about these hypothesized unseen parts of the Universe, and experiments that are designed to possibly "throw some light" on them. From here it moves deeper into theoretical zones, and looks at various "universal" proposals, from multiple-worlds to many-dimensioned realities, and discussing how these sorts of things might be approached on an experimental basis.

Finally, Halpern reviews some of the "horror story" scenarios that have appeared in the press (and on the web) since the start of the LHC, from creating a black hole that will swallow up the Earth, to supposed time-travel (it's a pity he didn't include how seeking out the mass of the Higgs Boson figures into the story line of the old SciFi series *LEXX*), putting them in contexts of being very very unlikely if not categorically impossible. A Conclusion at the end outlines some predictions for "The Future of High-Energy Physics", listing projects in the works, new technologies that might be arising, and the ever-gloomy look at the political will to fund these sorts of massive programs.

As you may have guessed, I thoroughly enjoyed reading Collider[4] and would recommend it to anyone who has an interest in physics, or even science in general. Not only is it a wonderful survey of what has happened in the field, it provides personalizing backgrounds on many major players that I'd never encountered previously, as well information on folks who did significant pieces of research that I'd never heard of. As this is brand-new, you should be able to find a copy at your local book vendor, although Amazon currently has it at a very substantial (35% off) discount. What I can't figure, though, is how "new" copies of this are already out in the "aftermarket" ... this is a wonderful popular science book, and deserves to find a wide audience!

Notes:

1. http://btripp-books.livejournal.com/95841.html
2. http://amzn.to/1Q7uYfQ
3. http://www.chicagonow.com/blogs/job-stalker/
4. http://amzn.to/1Q7uYfQ

Friday, July 16, 2010[1]

Digging it ...

Those regular readers who, perhaps, take a too-fine interest in what happens in this space may have noted that it's been an *awfully* long time since I read anything of an archaeological theme. The dynamics of my job search, both in keeping myself up-to-date with things Social Media based, and the on-going stream of unemployment-related books targeted for coverage in _The Job Stalker_[2], have put a definite damper on the amount of books that I would, all things being equal (and my being ensconced in a well-paying *job*), far prefer to read.

A few weeks back, however, there was a half-off sale at the very charming Open Books[3] (a used book vendor on the outer fringes of "my neighborhood" which is a fund-raising vehicle for a number of very worthy literacy programs), and I treated myself (and my daughters) to a few books. One of these was Michael D. Coe's authoritative _The Maya_[4], here in the "fully revised" Fourth Edition. While I had read other books by Coe, I'd somehow missed this one, and it was a treat to pick it up.

First of all, it is *lavishly* illustrated, with few pages not sporting some photo, chart, map, illustration, or hieroglyphic reproduction to bring home the points of the text. While I have both read a lot on the subject, and traveled extensively in the Yucatan, visiting many of the sites covered here (and spent many days at the *Museo Nacional de Antropología* in Mexico City, where much of the art, pottery, and carvings is housed), I was frequently amazed at some of the material that was unfamiliar to me (such as Stela D from Quiriguá Guatemala, which is *huge* at nearly 20' tall!) depicted here.

The book is largely structured chronologically, going from the earliest pre-civilized traces in the region, on up through the Conquest, when the glory years of Mayan culture were long gone, but the *people* still persevered (a condition that could well be argued is still the situation today in various parts of Mexico). One thing to note here is that Coe disciplines himself to really only be considering *the Maya*, cultures such as the Olmecs, while arguably the seed of Mayan (and other) cultures, are only dealt here to the extent that specific objects, words, and concepts found their way into the Mayan world. Similarly, the Toltec influence is only covered in terms of its *influence*, rather than as a separate group. One thing that I found fascinating here (and had *not* heard in numerous trips there), is a theory that the true seed of Mayan culture came from the Teotihuacan culture, suggesting a closer relation between the Mayan and Toltec cultures than just a later-period conquest of the former by the latter. One of the fascinating things in _The Maya_[5] is the use of maps to detail linguistic/cultural zones, political/cultural alignments, and migration/invasion routes for numerous groups in the area. Some of these seem, on the surface quite odd and unlikely, but do seem to be supported by both concrete and linguistic artifacts.

The closing section of the book is also interesting as it tries to frame "the world view" of the Maya, from their theology to cosmology, and their astronomy, number system, calendars, writing, etc. In the current anticipation (thanks to Arguelles and McKenna) of the "end of the Mayan calendar" in 2012 (although it's not "ending" any more than the western calendar "ended" in Y2K), there *was* a rather juicy bit here that I'm surprised has not been snatched up by the alarmists (especially in relation to recent world geological events) ... that the "fifth age" (our current one) is prophesied to be *destroyed by earthquakes*!

Anyway, this is a *splendid* book for learning about the Maya people and their culture, for both readers quite familiar with the subject, and ones who are just starting to become familiar with it. As noted, the copy I have here is the Fourth edition (from 1987), I see that the one currently in print is the *Seventh* edition (from 2005). The 4th is available from the new/used guys for very little, but if you're interested, you should probably go for the *newer* edition, as the field of Mayan studies has been going through very rapid growth over the past decades (especially in being able to read the glyphs), and so the later versions are likely far more useful read!

Notes:

1. http://btripp-books.livejournal.com/96224.html
2. http://www.chicagonow.com/blogs/job-stalker/
3. http://open-books.org/
4-5. http://amzn.to/1Q7tYZ8

Saturday, July 17, 2010[1]

I only wish it worked that way ...

OK, so here is another of those Review Copies sent to me by a publisher primarily because of my penning <u>The Job Stalker</u>[2] over on the Chicago Tribune's "Chicago Now" blog site (hellooooo FTC). What makes this book stand out (to me, at least) is that it's the first thing I've gotten from a publisher that came with *swag*. Now, I spent the majority of my career doing consumer product PR, and I know that you don't generally go through the expense of sending out the "cool stuff" to the riff-raff, so I had been feeling pretty puffed up having gotten a "KaChing" button (see the cover pic – it's like the Staples "easy" button, but it makes a sound like a cash register ringing) until being somewhat deflated to see that one could get one for free from the author's site. So, those of you worried that I've been "bought" ... well, there *was* a fun toy in play!

To be honest, I *have* recommended this book to folks I've spoken with while still reading it, but that's more due to its content than the fact that Wiley packaged it up with some swag. <u>KaChing: How to Run an Online Business that Pays and Pays</u>[3] is very much a *manual* for setting up shop on the Internet. Much more so than many of the books out there (several which have been featured in this space), this is a "how to" rather than a book on the "philosophy" of on-line selling. To its credit, it's far less "encyclopedic" than some, with the author, Joel Comm, pretty much talking about what has worked for him and folks he's associated with, and only presenting a few alternatives where there are multiple options.

Comm doesn't spend a lot of time navel-gazing here, instead he points the readers to the tools that are available (most for free and with very short learning curves), and tells them to get to it. This does bring me to one significant caveat, however, and one that I've discussed with other books (so it is a "me" thing and might not be a factor for *you* at all): one really needs to know what one "wants to do" (when one grows up or whatever). One has to focus on an area of expertise and make it monetizable ... an example of which would be *his Mother's* travel site, or another gal's Origami site. If you have an *identifiable passion* (which I, much to my on-going regret, appear to not), one can take the instructions in <u>KaChing</u>[4] and quickly turn it into an on-line business.

One other notable data point that kept grabbing my attention were the frequently *amazing* dollar amounts that get bandied about in here. If his book was a blog post, it is likely that it would fall afoul of the FTC guidelines for *generally expected performance* (Comm does go into this area quite a bit, but I guess without reflecting on the tone of the book), as the numbers discussed do generally trend towards the high side. Having been personally involved in *dozens* of web projects that had every intent of making money (and yet failed to find a paying audience) I took a lot of this "with a grain of salt".

Anyway, the book is structured in a walk-through of progressively more involved models, starting with a brief look at how resources are out there that would allow *anybody* to get up and running on the web, to how to find one's "niche" (and, again, this is where he loses me to a certain extent, as it's been my experience that niches and micro-niches simply mean vanishingly small populations with which to interact) and build a community in that, to the essential issue of content, which then leads to the area of "information products", selling these via affiliate programs, setting up membership sites, and developing coaching programs. Each of these is very step-by-step, with practical material all along the way (almost all of my bookmarks in this are for resources I'd not previously encountered).

As I noted above, I have already recommended KaChing[5] to a few people when conversations have turned to "I'd love to sell stuff on the Web", so my caveats above should not diminish the value I see in this book as a "manual" or reference. However, I've been kicking around e-commerce for 15 years, and I would warn the reader not to *expect* the sort of results suggested when Comm writes: *"Month after month, Google has been sending me checks for more than $15,000 each."* ... I'm guessing the "average" person really applying themselves to this in a reasonably popular niche is more likely to be seeing results closer to one percent of that figure. Of course, I've *failed* as much at this as Comm has *succeeded* so maybe you want to believe the upside, but be aware: you'll have to be talented, dedicated, and to a certain extent *lucky* to end up making a living off the web.

This is "hot off the presses", so should be available at your local brick-and-mortar book vendor, but Amazon has it at a 34% discount, which is usually your best bet for new releases. Again, I really enjoyed this book, thought it was very well organized, and felt the material it presented was top-notch ... but on a sour-grapes gut level from my own experiences, I still see what Comm has achieved as a "best case scenario", which leads me to temper what would otherwise be a solidly enthusiastic recommendation of the book.

Notes:

1. http://btripp-books.livejournal.com/96293.html
2. http://www.chicagonow.com/blogs/job-stalker/
3-5. http://amzn.to/1IGqRHd

Sunday, July 18, 2010[1]

If you can ...

For some reason I had been not getting around to reviewing this book for *ages* ... I'd picked it up (along with a whole bunch of web-based resources related to it) last *September* when its authors addressed the Social Media Club's monthly meeting. It took me a while to get into reading it, as I'd picked up their preceding The One Minute Millionaire[2] book on the theory that there would be a certain continuity between the two. I suppose this is, to some extent true. Mark Victor Hansen and Robert G. Allen's Cash In A Flash: Fast Money in Slow Times[3] bears both its predecessor's odd format (training material on the verso, "teaching story" on the recto) and focus on having "regular people" achieve their dreams through setting up their own businesses. The main difference was that, by the end of 2009, the real estate "magic bullet" that had been so strongly advocated in the previous book was no longer a serious option, and so there had to be a new route to all those dollars waiting just beyond the unenlightened seeker's reach.

Once again, in the "story" half, the participants faced a challenge, formed a working group, and managed to overcome the obstacles just in time, with various members achieving assorted levels of success, despite not necessarily having much belief in the process. Personally, this rings so amazingly hollow to me from what I've seen in *my* life experiences that the less said about the "novella" part of the book, the better. These and similar business "self-help" books always seem to advocate forming a "mastermind" group to achieve these sorts of beyond-belief goals. It has been my unwavering experience that anything that involves more than three people (and *that* dynamic is likely to have some dead weight) is going to get hopelessly political, bogged down in power struggles, and at *best* will have parts not carrying their load, and pissing off the ones who *are*. I'm sure that an idealized "dream team" would be very exciting and worthwhile, but one might as well wish for a goose that lays golden eggs.

Anyway, there are three "elements" to the "system" here ... the first being "Wow Now": forming a concrete vision of your "dreams" with the key phrase: *"Your dreams must be more real than your fears"*. This involves a lot of self-psyching (self-hypnosis?) with "higher vibration words", not using *any* "~~negative~~ not so positive" phrasing, and even re-writing how you remember your past. This is the "mind" part of the system, the next is the "heart" approach, which is the "Inner Winner", a name they give to "gut feelings", "intuitions", etc., in contrast to the "Inner Whiner" which listens to one's "critical voice". In this section there's a lot of exercising in journaling, self-analysis, etc., to find out what the "right" inner voice is talking about. Frankly, I found these first parts very well done, and despite the touchy-feely aspects, thought that this was quite worthwhile, and even wished there were *workshops* on this locally. However, the next part, the "Dream

Team", as noted above, might as well have been a section on how one needs to get Sasquatch, the Easter Bunny, Santa Claus, Nessie, and a couple of Leprechauns and Space Aliens together before becoming a success. I'd be *thrilled* to know a half a dozen people that I'd "trust with my back", but I've never met one in real life ... again, your experience with Humanity may be different, but this is where this (and other books like it) fall apart for *me*. Interestingly, they provide a 15-point questionnaire to "qualify" one's Dream Team members, but it's a list that I doubt that anybody (*myself* included) would be able to satisfactorily answer!

The last section of the book is called "Rapid Riches", and offers up thumbnail sketches of ways that one might (if they had the other three elements in place) attain the title's "Cash in a Flash". Again, I guess if you don't have the "Wow Now" mindset, the "Inner Winner" standing on the neck of the "Inner Whiner", and that ever-elusive "Dream Team" you're screwed. They break down these opportunities into "PSI": Products, Services, and Information, or, more informally, *stuff, doing stuff*, and *teaching others to do stuff*, although these seem to have centered on real estate (again, despite the market), and e-books. Well, I guess we discovered why it took me 9 months to do this review. I must admit that I *read* the book, and did *not* "work through the exercises" (as there were parts of those for which I have never had answers, so would likely still be frustratingly "stuck" there still). This also, obviously, pokes sharp sticks at very sore parts of my psyche, so do take into account how *you* handle this sort of stuff.

As noted, I bought Cash In A Flash[4] from the authors at a meeting, but it's sufficiently new (it came out last Fall) that it's likely to still be around at the brick-and-mortars. Amazon has it at about a third off, and their new/used guys have "very good" hardcover copies for under three bucks (plus S&H). Despite my "wailing and gnashing of teeth" above, I do feel this is a very good, albeit "newagey", sort of book that could very well help many people to find a way to making a new lifestyle. I know that there are protégés of Hansen & Allen out there who are (apparently successfully) pitching their own snake oil on late night TV, but I would be more enthused if there were *hundreds*, if not *thousands* of folks out there who were saying *"I did what they wrote and now have everything I ever dreamed of!"* ... caveat emptor, and all that ... this could be *the book* for you, if you happen to be the right person in the right situation with the right conditions ... I just don't think that *that* is me.

Notes:

1. http://btripp-books.livejournal.com/96569.html
2. http://btripp-books.livejournal.com/84923.html
3-4. http://amzn.to/1oYu0MR

Saturday, July 24, 2010[1]

In my kids' world ...

This book came to me via the "Early Reviewers" program over at LibraryThing.com[2], along with a request that, if possible, we push through the reviewing on it so that we could provide the LTER coordinator with questions for the author for a podcast that she's going to be producing the end of the month. As such, I had this jump ahead of several other things "in the queue" of my to-be-read pile.

Frankly, Rewired: Understanding the iGeneration and the Way They Learn[3] by Larry D. Rosen, Ph.D. seemed a bit of an odd book for me to get from the LTER program (whose "almighty algorithm" is supposed to closely match books with readers, based on their libraries), as it is very much targeted towards an "education" audience, examining issues which are primarily of interest to teachers and K-12 institutions. However, upon further reflection, it does make some sense as I am a father to two kids in the age group being discussed, and (as regular readers of these pieces will know) I've read quite a bit of new/social media material, as well as on-going looks at the technology involved. So, while not being part of the *target audience* per se, I'm at least an "informed outsider".

This book is ultimately a "call to action" for the educational community to begin to adjust teaching styles to the learning styles of various "generations", defined in Rosen's research as Baby Boomers (born between 1946 and 1964), Gen X (1965-1979), Net Gen (born between 1980 and the early '90s), and the new "iGen" kids born since the mid-1990's. Rosen's primary thesis is that this latter group has never known a "non-wired" world, and that their uptake and facility with technology has been both faster and more substantial than any of their predecessors.

Another key concept is that *"... most teens simply can't unitask. It's too slow and too quiet and too restricting."*, and Rosen argues that the traditional classroom modality is counter-productive in reaching these kids. It's not that they're just *resistant* to the classroom experience (what generation of kids *hasn't* preferred to be someplace other than in class?), but that their learning, social, and even perception styles are locked into a high-speed, technology-immersed, multi-tasking pattern which makes the linearity and "push" dynamic of the classroom nearly incomprehensible.

Rosen has a list of six aspects in which the "iGen" kids differ from preceding generations. They are strongly motivated by positive reinforcement, but this needs to be on-going, like achieving levels or goals in a video game and not in an end-of-semester assessment. They are, perhaps counter-intuitively, very focused on their family, and their connection with their parents. They are *very* confident, with figures from studies of this far surpassing previous generations (perhaps due to their mastery of available technologies). They are very open to change, flocking to innovations in huge numbers (the author attributes YouTube going from zero to fifty million views in a single year to their influence). They exhibit what Rosen calls "collective reflection", which is the product of nearly constant on-line and mobile communications between them and their "friends", who may be scattered globally. And, finally, they crave immediacy, the faster the information arrives, the better.

> They want to learn, but our current teaching models simply bore them to sleep. ... This is a generation that learns differently, and unless we recognize and accept those differences, we will turn them off to education.

Rosen develops some suggestions of ways that educational settings could be more immersive, and cites research which points to structures of cognitive processing which could function as a basis to these approaches. Of course, the main obstacle to all of this is that the *teachers* don't "live in the same world", and many are not only resistant to these concepts, but outright technophobic, and are uncomfortable to having "roles reversed" to get process-specific "tutoring" from kids half their age or younger.

One of the areas that Rosen sees the most promise in is the Virtual World environments such as Second Life. Moving educational experiences into these spaces would allow for many of the information-access modalities to be presented, while not *radically* re-working the actual school environment. He presents a 12-phase "model of technology implementation" that, used in conjunction with assessment tools such as "The Technology Skills, Beliefs, and Barriers Scale" should allow educational institutions to at least take the first steps into this new world.

As Rewired[4] is brand new, it is likely to be available via your local bookstore, however, given the relatively narrow focus, it might have to be ordered in. It's available (of course) online, with Amazon having it at about a third off of cover price. Since this seems to have been initially released in "mass market paperback" rather than in hardcover, the discounted cost is *quite* reasonable, so if you have an interest in education, information processing, generational differences, or cyber/mobile/virtual modalities, you might consider picking up a copy. While I understand that there is a certain level of controversy around this, it raises very interesting points, and I'm glad to have read it.

Notes:

1. http://btripp-books.livejournal.com/96964.html
2. http://btripp-books.com/
3-4. http://amzn.to/2OClPDH

Sunday, July 25, 2010[1]

This we could use!

This is probably the fastest turn-around that I've ever done on a review ... as the book in question just came in a couple of days ago, and I only decided that it might make an amusing entry for The Job Stalker[2] today. Fortunately (and, evidently), this was a quick read, and as I'm a scant 36 hours or so away from having a "bookless" Monday (which is usually my day for featuring job-search related books) on that blog, I'm now jumping into the review.

Those who have been reading my scribblings for any length of time will realize that this is *not* exactly "my sort of book", but given the gaping hole in my "review schedule" and the fact that it *is* (sort of) a job-search book, I figured cranking through this over the weekend would be a fun, productive exercise. This was sent to me from the nice folks at Ten Speed Press (who must have also figured that a "career" book was a "career book"), much to my amusement and that of my Daughters (the cats, however, don't much care for the concept). Careers For Your Cat[3], written by Ann Dziemianowicz and charmingly illustrated by Ann Boyajian, purports to be exactly what it sounds like, a way to get your kitty off its furry behind and out into the workforce.

> (what is) your freeloading, fat cat doing? ... I'll tell you what she *isn't* doing, she isn't raising one paw to help you. Nope. ... Your cat needs to get off the couch and get a job. Right now!

The book closely resembles (on some levels) the hundreds of "career counselor" books out there, but one penned by a cat specialist, with focus on the particular sorts of positions for which one's feline companions are particularly suited.

Pivotal to this effort is the "Meowers-Briggs Career/Personality Test" that one is directed to administer to your cat (I wonder how the Meyers-Briggs folks feel about this riff on their brand!). Part one of this consists of 16 multiple choice questions to determine if kitty exhibits "Creative", "Labor-Intensive", "Intellectual", or "Inert Introvert" traits (oh, plus one other, but I wouldn't want to spoil the fun). Part two is a brief quiz to determine if your cat is an "Introvert" or an "Extrovert", producing seven categories (obviously, if the kitty has "Inert Introvert" traits, they're unlikely to be an "Extrovert"). There are five careers suggested for each of the six combined attribute categories, with just four for those motion-adverse "InIs" (who are *"not made for jobs requiring stamina and endurance, or even standing up"*).

In each of the 30 "combined attribute" career paths that might be open to your feline freeloader, there are four specific attributes that the particular job requires (the "InIs" cats have just two each) that they'd "bring to the table", from an Interior Designer (a career for a "Creative Extrovert") who *"Can deconstruct a sofa on a moment's notice."* to a Pastry Chef (for the "Labor-Intensive Introvert") who *"Monitors food quality carefully."*, to the CEO (an "Intellectual Extrovert"), who is *"Clear about needs and wants."*, to the very sedentary "Inert Introvert" cat whose possible job as a Solar Technician *"Sets strong example as a passive solar collector."*.

There is a final section with do's and don't's for the job interview, with such key advice as *"Do not sit in the interviewer's lap."* and the essential *"Do not attempt any personal grooming at any time during the interview."*. Obviously, *War and Peace* this is not, but Careers For Your Cat[4] is an amusing, light read that it likely to appeal to anybody stuck in a job search, or stuck with do-nothing felines who could be out there helping with the family finances!

This book is not "officially" out for a week (I hope that Ten Speed doesn't mind me writing about this in advance), so your options for obtaining this are currently of the pre-order variety ... but it's supposed be hitting the stores on August 3rd, and I'm sure that your local brick-and-mortar book monger would be *happy* to reserve a copy for you.

Notes:

1. http://btripp-books.livejournal.com/97257.html
2. http://www.chicagonow.com/blogs/job-stalker/
3-4. http://amzn.to/1SaO5tQ

Saturday, July 31, 2010[1]

When gestures have meaning ...

Here's one of those "surprises" that came in from the folks at Wiley (helllooo, FTC). When this first came in, I was thinking "what am I supposed to do with *that*?", but because it was relatively short, and I'd hit a snag on another project (you'll hear about that eventually), I decided to slot it into my reading a week or so back. I was very happy that I did!

As long-time readers of my main blog space will recall, I used to be fairly active with my local Toastmasters group (before taking that job in Evanston in 2007). One of the things that seemed to be a challenge to even the most accomplished speakers, though, was body movement, and especially *congruent* body motions which enhanced your message delivery. Well, Sharon Sayler's What Your Body Says (And How to Master the Message): Inspire, Influence, Build Trust, and Create Lasting Business Relationships[2] (a remarkably bulky title for a book that runs only about 180 pages!) should definitely be on their reading list, as by following her basic set of instructions, most (especially new) speakers would have their presentations greatly improved.

Now, I have to confess that I have not *tried* practicing or implementing the suggestions in this book, but the general focus and direction of the material seems fairly plausible (I also have no idea how this might run counter or redundant to other "body language" books out there). However, the approach seems both reasonable and not particularly difficult to add to one's repertoire.

While there is quite a lot of material about how to "work a stage" in here, this is by no means a book "about public speaking", as a lot of it is targeted to small presentations, intimate groups, and even one-on-one situations. The main thrust here is to develop body language habits (primarily in the "what do I do with my hands?" ballpark) that will allow congruent messages in one's physical presence to match what one is *saying*. I don't know about you, but I am frequently taken aback when I see figures on TV who are clearly giving out two (or more) messages, and being able to avoid that in my *own* communications sort of hooked me on this book!

As I noted above, this is a fairly thin volume, and a non-negligible amount of that is involved in diagrams, tables, etc. One might think this would be a negative, but in this case it prevents the author from attempting to be "encyclopedic" and creates a fairly tight focus on hand/arm movements, stances, tone and pacing of voice, and a few other key elements. When one is done reading What Your Body Says[3] you will likely feel that you "have a handle on" this basic set of skills, know how to apply them, and are only a bit of practicing away from making their integral to one's communications skill set.

One of the things I found most fascinating here were the issues of *timing* of gestures, how and why to hold a hand position long, how to disassociate oneself with bad news, how to "change subjects" with motions, and similar practices. Here's a snippet on a related subject:

> *A verbal message has two parts: the actual spoken word and the silent pause between the segments, sentences, and thoughts. The silent pause allow the speaker to breathe. A silent, gestured pause allows the speaker to breathe and emphasize key parts of the message. Holding a gesture still (keep the same gesture, do not move it) throughout the pause allows the listener's mind to see, feel, interpret, and internalize the message, which adds more impact to the verbal message.*

The first part of the book discusses the concept of "signals", what they are, how they work, why they influence one's audience, etc. This then moves into several chapters on types of gestures, "Gestures of Relationship", "Gestures of Location", "Gestures That Teach", and "Gestures of Expectation and Influence", each of which is broken down into sub-sections on specific elements of these general areas. She then covers material about the eyes, and the voice, and then how to pull all the various bits together. Again, this is fairly brief and to-the-point, so there's lots of things condensed into this limited space.

This is brand-new (in fact, I just noticed that its official release date is August 2nd), so you should be reasonably successful in finding it at any general-interest local book vendor. Amazon, of course, has it at about 1/3rd off the cover price, which is probably your cheapest option (bizarrely, some of the new/used guys have copies of this already, but many have it priced higher than Amazon does!). If you are a communicator, be it on stage, on video, in meetings, in groups, etc., I suspect that you will find this a *very* useful book, and if you're in Toastmasters, I think this will likely give your presentations a big jump in effectiveness. Again, it's just me, but I'd not encountered as compact and "easy to implement" guide book on going for body/speech congruency before this, so I'm pretty enthusiastic about it.

Notes:
1. http://btripp-books.livejournal.com/97528.html
2-3. http://amzn.to/1oYrAhp

Sunday, August 1, 2010[1]

I'd love to go there ...

This is another book that I picked up at the sale they were having at my new favorite almost-in-my-neighborhood used book store Open Books[2] (which is part of their fund-raising efforts for a wide array of very worthy literacy programs) a few weeks ago. Back when I had money (in my P.R. Executive days) I used to do a lot of "archaeological travel", and this book jumped off the shelf at me for being about one of the top-of-my-list locations that I've not been fortunate enough to visit (sadly, the "want to visit" list is much deeper than my "been there" list).

Unfortunately, I found Angkor: Temples of Cambodia's Kings[3] somewhat lacking on what I was looking for in a book on the fabled Cambodian site. There are a few odd things about this volume, for one, the author's name, Dawn F. Rooney, does not appear on the cover, and there is a photographer credited (Michael Freeman) in a book that is *largely* missing current photography (not that there isn't a good deal of photos in here, just that most of them are from early expeditions in the 1800's).

Now, I'll grant that what I was hoping this book to be, and what this book actually was, were diverging due to no particular fault of its own. I was anticipating that this would be one of those "visit the site from your armchair" sorts of books that walks you through with descriptions and images in close collaboration. Instead, this ends up being very much more oriented to folks on-site, telling the reader what to find where at which of the ruins, with very little "showing" involved.

If you're not familiar with the Angkor area (more generally referred to as just one of the ruins, Angkor Wat), it is an *amazing* and sprawling site in the south-east Asian jungle. The main site is about 15 by 5 miles in size, with two massive artificial lakes framing it, each being approximately *five miles long* by about 2 miles wide, and austerely rectangular. A while back I was messing around with Google Maps to take a look at various ruin sites around the planet, when I found Angkor Wat, I was *shocked* by those features, as I had always thought of this as the one ruin area (itself a respectable square mile or more), and was unaware of it being part of a much larger complex of ruins. The French were instrumental in most of the research and rebuilding of these sites, from the mid-1800's up until the chaos of the Pol Pot regime, which threw out all foreigners in 1972. It was only in relatively recent years that Angkor was again accessible to Western visitors.

The book is structured in three parts, "Background", covering geography, history, religion, architecture and art, "The Monuments" which describes in various detail several dozen sites (in alphabetical order), and a section of appendices and other reference materials. I would certainly recommend the first part of the book to anyone with interest in the Khmer culture, as it is a very well developed combination of materials which provide in 60 or so pages a quite satisfactory over-view of the subject. The site arose in a fairly compact slice of time, from the mid-800's for the earliest monuments through the mid-1200's, but there was quite a lot of change within in that, with various influences (Indian, Chinese, and local) coming to bear, which is reflected in the evolving styles (Hindu, Buddhist, etc.) in the different sites.

The "meat" of the book, however, is in the site-by-site discussion. Again, this is where I was disappointed, as the author *writes* about all sorts of fascinating things that the visitor should look at, but there are almost no *pictures* associated with these descriptions to bring it to life. Each has a detailed "site plan" showing the lay-out, and in some cases suggested routes to take when one's there, but for those of us on *this* side of the planet, that doesn't help much! This is, of course, my wanting the book to be something that it's not ... the material here is certainly *informative*; there is an introduction for each site, giving Location in relation to the over-all region, Access in terms of how best to approach the site, Tips if these are needed for which side might have easier climbs, etc., Date of the monument, Kings who were in power when it was built, Religion that is expressed in the design, and Art Style as these developed. The text then goes into a background on each, and then discusses the layout, sometimes in very fine detail. I only wish that there were several photos of each of these to go with the text ... what modern photos there are tend to be divorced from the context of the copy.

It does appear that Angkor[4] is out of print. The copy I have is the 1994 edition, which seems to have been updated and expanded in a 2001 edition, both of which are only available via the used channels. However, there are copies of the later version going for as little as $0.14 (plus shipping, of course), so if this sounds like something you'd enjoy (and, really, it is quite a decent resource, just not the "vacation in a book" that I was hoping for), it's out there.

Notes:

1. http://btripp-books.livejournal.com/97683.html
2. http://open-books.org/
3-4. http://amzn.to/1VjlXJf

Friday, August 6, 2010[1]

Stealth fundie spew ...

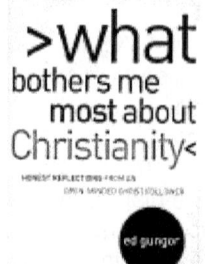

This is one of those books that I "won" over in Librarything.com's "Early Reviewer" program. I was, frankly, surprised when this showed up, as it was *fourteen months late*, having been a May 2009 selection that did not show up until July 2010. They really shouldn't have bothered. All the info on the book made it sound like it was a Christian struggling with various obvious "issues" one might have with Christianity, but it really is simply a bible-thumping evangelical using these "sore points" to flog bible quotes on the unsuspecting reader. There has been several instances where Fundie presses like Howard Books have "snuck into" the LTER listings with "secular" descriptions ... I'm disappointed that Simon & Schuster (who recently acquired Howard) would allow this sort of deceit, as it reflects *very* badly on the whole corporation.

Anyway, fundamentalist preacher Ed Gungor's What Bothers Me Most about Christianity: Honest Reflections from an Open-Minded Christ Follower[2] is hardly what somebody from outside the glassy-eyed flock would consider "honest reflections" ... the description given to LTER readers led with this: *"with candor, reason, and humor, Gungor addresses ten tough issues of Christianity"*, except that he really *doesn't*. This is less what bothers him most *about Christianity* and more him struggling with points of history, doctrine, or behavior *for which he doesn't have easy answers*. At NO point does he allow consideration that the Bible is not the inerrant Word Of God, so what is really "bothering" him is that there are a lot of things which require excessive amounts of mental convolution to fit in with approved doctrine. On many levels this book reminds me of the "trolls" on-line who sweep into variously un-related chat rooms, spew something about biblical inerrancy and then proceed to "witness" until banned. While reading this book I was frequently wishing I had an eject/ban button to use on Rev. Gungor!

So, you want to know what "bothers" him about Christianity? Here's the list:

> "It bothers me that God is intentionally hiding."
> "It bothers me that reason alone doesn't lead to faith."
> "It bothers me that God allows evil in the world."
> "It bothers me that Jesus is the only way to a relationship with God."
> "It bothers me that science and faith sometimes seem incompatible."
> "It bothers me that so many Christians give Christianity a bad name."
> "It bothers me that Gods looks like such a bully in the Old Testament."
> "It bothers me that believers consistently misuse sacred text."
> "It bothers me that the Christian faith includes a hell."

I don't suppose it would surprise anybody that he manages to perform enough convolutions and cherry-pick enough quotations to finally justify these all to some degree of (his) satisfaction, no matter how recursive and/or "convenient" that justification might be.

I will credit Rev. Gungor with at least *raising* certain issues, if to only to eventually smother them. I'm sure that within the author's flock, even *admitting* to these questions being "issues" is "edgy" bordering on "dangerous". He even, from time to time, comes up with perfectly lucid commentary such as:

> *Christian leaders began to justify using torture to keep heretics from gaining influence in the church. A heretic was anyone who held a theological or religious opinion or doctrine that was contrary to the orthodox doctrine of Christianity. This was extended to include opinions about philosophy, politics, science, art, and the like.*

Or...

> *the Bible should come with a warning label slapped on its cover: "If you are already kind of nuts, this book will only make things worse"*

One actually *useful* concept he uses here is what he calls "Blueblockers" (named for the as-seen-on-TV sunglasses that he used to wear which caused him to have a hard time perceiving color differences), which he then spins out to how so many people interpret biblical injunctions in terms of *their* cultural biases. As telling as this is in the examples that he gives, he is never able or willing to take *the next step* and look askance at the Bible itself ... in each of the chapters he ends with a barrage of justification that pretty much says "oh, it's OK", no matter how offensive the "bothersome" subject was.

Again, I'm very likely NOT the audience for which this book was intended (despite its publisher sneaking it into the LTER), I'm sure that this would be a "challenging" (bordering on *titillating* for positing "dangerous ideas") read for the sorts of Christians whose faith is a string of fairy-tale platitudes bolstered by reinforcing group-think ... sort of a roller-coaster ride that toyed with heresy but brought everybody back safely away from the hazards of questioning at the end. As noted above, this is more about being bothered that the author doesn't have *easy answers* to this string of quite valid questions (which he at times, as in the science vs. religion section, can't even frame accurately) and he ends up weaving a toddler's blankie of biblical quotations that's just enough to get everybody back to sleep.

Needless to say, I wouldn't recommend this to anybody outside of the Fundamentalist/Evangelical camp. If you have functioning rational mentation, this religious contortionist side-show will only serve to irritate ... however, if you have relatives of the *"What about the BABY JESUS?!"* ilk, this would make a *lovely* gift, one which might just seed some REAL questions! To this end, I'll note that Amazon has a "bargain price" edition at 80% off of cover, which would be your best bet for picking this up.

Notes:
1. http://btripp-books.livejournal.com/97985.html
2. http://amzn.to/1StPgSo

Saturday, August 7, 2010[1]

Yes, a non-boring book on business ...

A couple of months back, I was at an event down at OfficePort[2] where Jason Fried was one of the presenters. His (with David Heinemeier Hansson and illustrations by Mike Rohde) Rework[3] had just come out, and he was doing a talk largely based on the book, with graphics in the same style. I'd been intending on picking up a copy, especially as so many of the bloggers, tweeters, and other online commentators were so enthusiastic about it, but due to its popularity, copies were not shaking out into the used market at any significant discount (and, being now in the 15th month of my current job search, "significant discounts" are the only situations in which I'm comfortable shelling out any of the rapidly dwindling resources I have). Fortunately, Amazon came up with this at nearly half off, and I pulled the trigger on it a few weeks back.

Rework[4] is an odd book on a lot of levels. For one, its copyright page, usually appearing on the verso of the title page or a few sheets back from there, is here on page 280, the *last* thing in the book. No explanation or commentary about this appears ... it's just that way. Plus there *is* no title page, the book starts with two pages of laudatory blurbs and then launches into a table of contents. Again, "odd". I had also not anticipated that it was going to be as "heavily illustrated" as it was, with poster-like (or marker-on-whiteboard like) full-page graphics accompanying each 1-3 page section here. I guess I hadn't flipped through this when it came in, as this came as a surprise when I decided to take this with me on a jaunt up to Daughter #1's new school, which (due to a "communication breakdown") involved my having to wait for 3 hours, during which I managed to pretty much complete the entire book!

This is almost more of a "revolutionary pamphlet" addressing the business world than a book. It is split up into a dozen "chapters" each having one to twelve sections. The chapters include "Go", "Progress", "Productivity", "Competitors", "Evolution", "Promotion", "Hiring", "Damage Control", and "Culture", with various lessons that Fried has learned from his years of running the very successful 37Signals[5] software company. One might argue what Fried and his associates have managed there might not be applicable everywhere, but in Rework[6] he at least provides something of a conceptual blueprint for putting a new paradigm of business into play.

One telling point appears in the "Build half a product, not a half-assed product" section of the "Progress" chapter: *"We cut this book in half between the next-to-last and final drafts. From 57,000 words to about 27,000 words. Trust us, it's better for it."* ... later in that chapter, in the "Sell your by-products" segment, they note that this book is a by-product, and one wonders where the other half of this that was dropped will end up!

Fried certainly sounds like he's "walking his talk", but his talk isn't necessarily something that is easy to take (I recall that I found the presentation I heard him give quite aggravating in parts), and I doubt that many can read through this without having *some* of their "sacred cows" gored. I know that I bristled at some of *my* "standard operating procedures" being shot down in the interest of various points here (as a life-long PR guy, having press releases being categorically called "spam" was an irritation, and the suggestion that "foregoing sleep is a bad idea" prompted me to wonder how *he* got the luxury of 36-hour days!).

Of course, for every one segment that I disagreed with on some level, there were two which I was thrilled to see, from "Planning is guessing" (take *that* MBA's!) to the charming "Don't scar on the first cut" section, which reads:

> Policies are organizational scar tissue. They are codified overreactions to situations that are unlikely to happen again. They are collective punishment for the misdeeds of an individual.
>
> This is how bureaucracies are born. No one sets out to create a bureaucracy. They sneak up on companies slowly. They are created one policy – one scar – at a time.

And, needless to say, for a guy who has occasionally taken flak for the "conversational" tone of these reviews and my other blogging efforts, the "Sound like you" section in the "Culture" chapter comes across as a ringing endorsement.

Given that Rework[7] is new, and very popular, it is likely to be available pretty much everywhere you can find books. I am hardly alone in my hearty recommendation of this, as it's a breath of fresh air in the world of "business books". As noted, Amazon is featuring this at a 42% discount, which puts it in the same price-point zone as even the used copies, which means that you pretty much don't have a good excuse for *not* picking up a copy!

Notes:

1. http://btripp-books.livejournal.com/98114.html
2. http://officeportnetwork.com/locations/
3-4. http://amzn.to/1S5DxMw
5. http://37signals.com/
6-7. http://amzn.to/1S5DxMw

Sunday, August 8, 2010[1]

Difficult to read, but thought-provoking ...

Calm down. This is a book that I read *last November*, and have been putting off reviewing ever since. Why? Well, as any reader of this space knows, I have been in a seemingly *unending* job search, and "common wisdom" would have it that when one is being eye-balled by potential employers one must be as vanilla as possible, purging all controversy, weakness, and *attitude* from one's on-line presence, as those HR folks out there are looking for ANY excuse to round-file an application. I can't even begin to tell you what a frustration this has been, as in following this "wisdom" I have stripped away nearly everything which is identifiably "me" in favor of a mask which is as close as I can approach to "ideal employee drone". I *hate* this (ooh, one of those no-no words!) but it's the reason that over most of the past year, my personal blog has been so non-personal: I do book reviews, I talk about my posts over on The Job Stalker[2] and rarely dare to profess any opinions beyond something I have enjoyed (or not) in my now-rare ventures into a restaurant. However, a combination of this being the *only* thing left in my to-be-reviewed pile and the encouragement I found in Jason Fried's Rework[3], I'm going ahead and reviewing this.

Yes, I realize that Glenn Beck is "the new Ann Coulter", the media figure that's most likely to make liberal/leftists' heads explode with uncontrolled indignation. Sorry. I'm certainly hoping that anybody considering my resume isn't going to jettison my application due to my not parroting the Big Brother-esque groupthink "hate" against Mr. Beck, although I recognize that in a lot of contexts, this sort of conformity of opinion (non-profits, I'm looking at you), is *de rigueur*, and that any variance from the "party line" demands extreme response.

That being said, Glenn Beck's Glenn Beck's Common Sense: The Case Against an Out-of-Control Government, Inspired by Thomas Paine[4] is not a particularly easy book to get through. I am a long-time Libertarian, and no fan of big government, or government involvement in commerce or individuals' personal lives, but Beck's view of the world is so *grim*. The essential take-away from Beck's half of this book (oh, one thing that came as a surprise here was that 55 pages out of a 175-page book was a reprint of Thomas Paine's *Common Sense*, a wonderful, and *essential* read, but a "subtraction by addition" in the context of this volume) is that we, as Americans, are *totally screwed*, and that we are on a course to a dystopia that is likely to look like mid-50's Albania writ large.

I don't suppose that this will be much of a surprise to any who have watched Beck's show on Fox over the past many months ... he has the emotional presence of a man who has had his dearest love given a dire prognosis, and is desperate to find a way to reverse the illness. Perhaps I'm some sort of Pollyanna on this, perhaps I'm delusional, perhaps I just don't want to look as deeply into the maw of the beast as Beck does, but I still think that we can pull away from the Statist death spiral that has dragged the country down over the past several years. However, Beck walks the reader through a truly nightmare scenario here, a darkness that America is unlikely to crawl out of, at least in any form that would be recognizable *as America*.

Beck, does, however, provide one very useful bit of conceptualization here, and that is defining the struggle not being between left and right, liberal and conservative, or even statist and libertarian, but between "PROGRESSIVES" and those who still hold to the vision of the Founding Fathers. This was something of a "lightbulb moment" for me, as it has been a long time since I was able to be even moderately enthusiastic about prominent Republicans, only voting that way out of disgust for the vermin typically representing the Democratic Party. Beck has a great description of this (especially in light of the 2008 election):

> *The Progressives on the right believed in Statism and American expansion through military strength, while the Progressives on the left believed in Statism and expansion through transnationalist entities such as the League of Nations and then the United Nations. ... Progressivism is why, with few exceptions, Americans feel though the candidates they get to choose from are pretty much the same. Do you elect Progressive candidate A or <u>really Progressive</u> candidate B?*

Unfortunately, Beck has the same failing as many of those who would call out the Progressives, the insistence on bringing his "imaginary friends" into the discussion. The main thing that drove me from the Republican Party and into the arms of the Libertarians was the "dominionist" slant which exhibited itself in such madness as forcing Bush Sr. to accept Dan Quayle as his VP ... while Beck is a Mormon convert, this same sort of anti-rational vibe is front-and-center (well, it's #2 on the list) in his "9-12 Project", which he posits as the counter-balance to the Progressive destruction of America. Why can't America have a non-Statist, non-Religious, rationality-based 3rd option?

Anyway, this is a book that *should* be read by many, but is only likely to be read "by the choir"; and for some, like me, it's a difficult thing to accept. Between Glenn Beck's Common Sense[5] being relatively recent (2009) and the notoriety of the author, it is likely to be available at most larger bookstores (unless "purged" by left/liberal employees, as is frequently the case). However, if you don't want to get into a fight with the commissar behind the counter, you can get this from Amazon for under ten bucks. Again, it's not a fun read, but it is an *eye-opening* review of what has gone wrong with America, and on that basis, I'd suggest it for those willing to take the effort to chip the gems out of the matrix.

Notes:

1. http://btripp-books.livejournal.com/98504.html
2. http://www.chicagonow.com/blogs/job-stalker/
3. http://btripp-books.livejournal.com/98114.html
4-5. http://amzn.to/1StKUKW

Friday, August 13, 2010[1]

More than meets the eye ...

This is a profoundly strange book. Not strange as in being thematically or stylistically bizarre, but strange as in making one wonder *why* it exists. F. Gonzalez-Crussi's <u>On Seeing: Things Seen, Unseen, and Obscene</u>[2] is one of those books that found its way into my hands through a clearance sale, in this case last year's haul from the $1.99 books on B&N's site. When shopping in this context, I find myself paging though many hundreds of books looking for things which seem "interesting" ... frequently, I'm reaching out into literary niches that I am not overly familiar with, in an effort to reach the magical "free shipping zone" to maximize my discount (I just got another 13 from this year's sale, and paid about $28 for somewhere around $188 worth of books, at original cover price).

This is a collection of essays considering (as one would surmise from the title), issues of *seeing*, *sight*, *vision*, etc. Its author is a Professor Emeritus in Pathology at Northwestern University Medical School who has published previous volumes on anatomy, the senses, and other vaguely medical concerns. This book, while being "on seeing", is not medical, but is more the philosophical musings of a venerable figure whose estimable career has put him in a position where enough people care to hear what he has to say that he's able to produce a volume like this.

Now, I fear that I'm sounding too negative about this book ... I don't mean to, as it is quite well written, and certainly interesting within its scope, but it's *odd*. It begins with a discussion entitled *"Female Genitals: Men's Foremost Visual Taboo"*, which is anchored on the telling of a story from the French Revolution, and wends its way to the convoluted history of the near-pornographic image of Gustave Courbet's painting *The Origin of the World* via the Greek myth of Actaeon and Diana and eventually to modern performance artists such as Annie Sprinkle (and this is just the first chapter).

The book then moves into a look at the historical *toilet* and birthing rituals of the Royalty of various cultures, which then spins off into a discussion of the totemic aspects of Kings and Queens, and how they must constantly *be seen*, and then using this as a filter to consider the current merchandising of fame. The next chapter first notes how little previous societies cared about the inner functioning of the body (despite, like the Aztecs, having plenty opportunities for internal observation), which then shifts to considering the (dead) body from the outside, and a rather extensive discussion of the Paris Morgue in the last century, which operated as a public spectacle, with tens of thousands of visitors coming through *a day* when notable or particularly gruesome deaths had been in the papers!

The book looks more at art, at executions, and at medical procedures, shifting back and forth through time, through chapters with assorted nominal themes. One page may be delving into mythology, while another a few turns later will be discussing surgical procedures, and the next musing on the nature of the media. While being an eclectic educational experience, it's quite a whirl, at times almost hallucinogenic (a video version of this would certainly manifest that way!), and moves from one chapter subject to the next in a cyclonic overlay of lurid imagery, historical vignettes, and contemplations on the human condition. Gonzalez-Crussi finally "brings this home" in the final chapter, which deals with microscopy, pathology, and his own background (as a Mexican physician), but, again in a mélange of levels and thematic expositions.

This is all fascinating, of course, as the author brings in a nearly encyclopedic knowledge to his subject matter, but on the whole, On Seeing[3] doesn't go anywhere ... it's a trip down a particularly framed rabbit hole, which leaves the reader chanting "curiouser and curiouser" like a mantra in trying to figure out what they've just absorbed.

Oddly enough (given that I'd acquired this via a $1.99 *clearance* sale), On Seeing[4] appears to still be in print, so would be available out there if you felt like taking this particular trip ... Amazon has it for *less* than half-price at the moment, however, and there are copies available via the new/used vendors for as little as 1 cent (plus the shipping, of course). This would certainly appeal to those with omnivorous intellectual tastes, and would be an *informative* read for anybody, but it's a deeply strange book, which is very hard to nail down as a particular recommendation ... I liked it well enough, and perhaps you might too.

Notes:

1. http://btripp-books.livejournal.com/98721.html

2-4. http://amzn.to/1NI1cVe1

Monday, August 16, 2010[1]

No, not like THAT ...

This is another of the review-copy books I've gotten (from the good folks at Wiley, if the FTC's listening) of late that seem to be focusing on, if not *networking* per se, at least elements that would go into successful networking. Frankly, this one's a bit of an odd duck, being more of a coaching book on getting what you want in business contexts, with a "30-day plan" for skill building in that area.

The Art of Business Seduction: A 30-Day Plan to Get Noticed, Get Promoted, and Get Ahead[2] was written by Mark Jeffries, a former Merrill Lynch stockbroker, who found himself in need of a new profession back in the 90's, and managed to reinvent himself as a broadcaster, speaker, and communications consultant. As one would surmise from the sub-title, this is centered around a month-long self-training program which purports to bring one up to speed on what Jeffries refers to as his *"surefire four-step process – L-WAR"* (and, I hate to say it, there is a certain tone that hovers over this that brings to mind the classic Veg-o-matic TV pitches at times).

What *is* "Business Seduction", you ask? Well, it's not about the cougar in the C-suite or the eye-candy down in IT ... so get your mind out of the gutter!

> *"The lessons you'll learn from this book will train you how to get noticed for the right reasons by the right people. ... The art of business seduction frees you to effortlessly connect with and influence others so that they not only come to believe that they want you and the services you offer, but even more impressive, they'll believe they need you for their own success."*

What is "L-WAR"? Simply the framework of Listen, Watch, Anticipate, and React. The 30-day program here is largely to get one into the habit of implementing the first two of these in a conscious and systematic way, which is then followed with suggestions of how to effectively do the latter two. When I noted above the "odd duck" nature of this, it's largely due to this "main part" of the book only taking up the first half. It suggests that Jeffries might have initially have intended "The Art of Business Seduction" to be a pay-to-download e-book, but that it got a bit long for that format ... certainly the self-promotional over-tones here would be perfectly at home in those "squeeze pages" hawking the thousands of .pdf tomes out there which promise to enlighten the purchaser on any number of topics! I can imagine a scenario where an e-book project got sold to a regular publisher, on the basis on it being fleshed out to a more respectable "dead tree volume" length (in this case an even 200 pages).

While the "30-Day Plan" here certainly has *value* and appears to be a plausible approach to making one a more influential person, it's the *second half* of the book that I, personally, found the must useful information. From the "Networking Secrets" chapter, "The Five Stages of Successful Networking" (Establishing Trust, The Sell, The Promise, The Release, and The Follow-up) was of particular note, with one part of "The Sell" standing out, his discussion of "The Jealousy Reaction", which is a subtle way of seeding in previous achievements that makes the person you're talking with suddenly feel they're missing out without your services!

There are other sections here on one's voice, appearance, and electronic communications, and one's "elevator pitch", but none of these offer any great revelations to most folks, I'd think. There is also quite a bit about "reading body language" (of exactly the sort avoided in a previous book[3] reviewed in this space) sprinkled through the book. Again, *my* reaction when getting half-way through this was to think *"that's it?"* and a lot of the rest does seem a bit like "filler". However, between the core "L-WAR" material and the *very* valuable Networking chapter (itself taking up nearly a quarter of the page count), there is quite a lot here to recommend this.

The Art of Business Seduction[4] is brand new (being released last month), so it will no doubt be available at your larger brick-and-mortar book vendors, and orderable via the rest. As usual, the on-line guys have it at a discount, and a few copies are kicking around the used channel (although at no great price break, you'd probably do as well to get it new as part of an Amazon/B&N order with free shipping). Again, this seemed useful *enough*, but with the caveats noted above ... its core concepts are dealing with social/business skills that would be helpful to anybody, but (to *my* reading) it's got "issues" that might have not been so glaring with some more aggressive editing.

Notes:

1. http://btripp-books.livejournal.com/98857.html
2. http://amzn.to/1S5zAHG
3. http://btripp-books.livejournal.com/97528.html
4. http://amzn.to/1S5zAHG

Saturday, August 21, 2010[1]

OOOPS ...

I need to confess a transgression here. I did something with this book that I almost *never do*, I went off and checked out a number of reviews in the middle of reading it. My intent was fairly honorable, as I was wanting to find some "historical" context for why this was as familiar to me as it was when I saw a copy at my new favorite used book store, OpenBooks[2], a month or so back, but what I read almost made me tempted to just not bother finishing it. *Mea culpa*. Obviously, having done this results in a *totally* different set of impressions than I would have had were I to have simply read through the book and set into doing my review, and *then* seeing what the rest of the world thought of it. Oops.

Anyway, Mutant Message Down Under[3] is something of a "newage classic", and the copy I picked up is from 1991, when the author, Marlo Morgan, was still both self-publishing it, and claiming it to be a true story (it was since picked up by a major publisher and reclassified as "fiction"). One of the reasons that I went to check the "lineage" of the book is that, back in the 80's and 90's, I did a *lot* of "metaphysical travel" and I have read a good number of books which others have generated from their experiences in strange settings around the world, and I was curious as to how this might have related to the rest of that genre.

This is the (admittedly, rather implausible) story of a 50-something woman suddenly finding herself in the company of a totally non-acculturated Aboriginal tribe on a many-month "walkabout" in the Australian outback. Now, as I've read many books along these lines, I'm used to a certain level of implausibility on the set-up, and outright "fictionalization" of events that, in some cases, I was actually witness to (making somewhat confusing reads for me of some friends' books!). However, the story here starts with a scenario requiring a *huge* level of "suspension of disbelief", with the author being under the impression that she was being picked up at her hotel to go to an *awards banquet* in her honor (for a program she'd organized for urban Aboriginal youth), in heels, jewelry, etc., and is instead driven for hours in an open jeep into the desert where all of her clothing and belongings are summarily dumped in a fire, and she is "tested" variously, and then led out into the searing heat with no headgear, and a simple native dress ... this with no total freak-out.

I don't really want to get into the specific points of unlikelihood here (there are plenty of sources to look that up, if you care to), but her story is that she had some "mystic connection" with this particular (unknown to anybody else) tribe, and that she managed to survive what would (from conditions she described) have likely killed most, White *and* Aboriginal, and that she was taken to their most sacred, secret (again, a place described with details that stretch credulity), locations where she (and only she) is given the Big Message to take back to the "Mutants" (that would be us). Again, had I not read so many pieces relating to this book, I wouldn't have incriminating details of her real biography to cross-reference against what's in the book, so I'm probably being more cynical here than I would have been were I just to have read this without that other data.

As is the case in many books of this kind, there *are* points that are *fascinating*, but aside from Ms. Morgan's say-so, there's precious little corroborating material for almost *any* teaching, method, practice, or activity she attributes to her tribal hosts. In fact, representatives of an Aboriginal association made the effort to travel to the U.S. to confront her about this and managed to get the book re-framed as "fiction" (no doubt deeply cutting into her business of marketing "teachings" of "The Mutant Message"). This is one of those books that one *wishes* were true in several parts … and it's been my experience that sometimes *real* "hidden secrets" do sometime manage to come through in even the most "fluff bunny" books, so *maybe* there might be a few grains of metaphysical truths scattered in here, but I'm afraid the evidence looks like this is popular more for its readers "wanting to believe" rather than there being anything substantial here *to* believe in.

This does seem to still be in print, in a later paperback edition, so it's "out there", but I can hardly advise "going retail" in this case. If your curiosity is piqued, however, hundreds of copies of the *hardcover* edition of the Harper version are in the new/used channels, with dozens of "very good" copies for 1¢ (plus the $3.99 shipping, of course), so that's probably your best bet!

Notes:

1. http://btripp-books.livejournal.com/99126.html
2. http://open-books.org/
3. http://amzn.to/1XrkKwG

Sunday, August 22, 2010[1]

If you can define your goal ...

Every now and again I end up reading a book that I *should* be very enthusiastic about, but just can't connect with. This, unfortunately, appears to be one of those. I do want to put my following comments in context, however, because it's pretty clear that the majority of my issues with this are arising on *my* end, and not due to particular faults with the book (although it certainly doesn't offer up much of any assistance to folks like me). Well Connected: An Unconventional Approach to Building Genuine, Effective Business Relationships[2] by career coach Gordon S. Curtis (a review copy of which was provided to me by the Jossey-Bass division of Wiley) is a book about refining one's networking strategies to achieve one's business goals. Now, as anyone who has been following this space (and my other blogs) will know, I've been in a long-term job search, and attend networking events 2-4 times a week, so the *concept* of the book caught my attention, and networking within a job search *is* one of the scenarios directly addressed here.

The book charts out the author's "Right Person – Right Approach" method, which is designed to put the individual in control of the information flow, finding the "critical enablers" who have the information that one needs to get to one's targets. The primary elements of this are:

- Clearly articulate your objective – learn how to identify and measure both the micro and macros objectives so your audience always knows what you are asking and how to help.
- Identify the critical enabler – develop an "unfair advantage by locating not only exactly what type of intelligence or relationship you need, but who best to get it from.
- Provide the right gesture of reciprocity – position yourself in a way that your critical enablers not only agree to talk to you out of obligation, but *are motivated to help you*.

Rather than simply walk the reader through these steps, the author "personalizes" these with stories of several dozen people using his method in a wide range of contexts which help to illustrate what might be a "critical enabler" in various situations. There are some key factors, however, to this elusive contact: they must be *knowledgeable*, they must feel *obligated* to assist you, and *motivated* to actually render that aid; additionally, they must have the *inclination* to be helpful, exhibit *availability* to be able to help, and ideally have a degree of *like-mindedness* to help cement the connection.

All this is great for people who know what they want. I frequently use the example that were I an accountant, and was looking for work in a certain type of accounting firm, I'd have no problem defining my objectives, macro or micro ... however, I have *dozens* of potential job categories in which I'm experienced and that I *could do*, and (depending on situational elements) be equally happy doing ... yet I have *never* been able (despite years of trying) to narrow things down much beyond defining the things that I know that I *wouldn't* be good at or want to do! Unfortunately, this would appear to put me into a category that the author somewhat "washes his hands of":

> I'd say that not truly being able to articulate their objectives – which translates to not knowing how to describe what they want clearly enough to get help – is the single most glaring shortcoming people face.

This quote surfaces at *the very end* of the book ... there is no "help" here, no "system" for those suffering this "shortcoming", although he *empathizes*, saying *"I find it painful to watch so many people beating their heads against the wall"* ... but if you can't get past the "objectives" phase, you are pretty much not going to be able to use his method! The perception of this was a cloud hanging over the entire book as I read it, and was not (as noted) even addressed as a *condition* until the last few pages. I found myself thinking "well, this might be great in a one-on-one consulting situation (in which this elusive "objective" might be wrested from dark recesses of my psyche), but how do you get to that *first* step?" ... and there really *isn't* anything addressing this in the book. Again, that's *me*, but I think it's a significant caveat when considering Well Connected[3] ... if you know *what you want*, this is a *great* book, but if your objectives are as vague as "I want a well-paying job doing something that I'm good at in a stimulating environment where my contributions are appreciated" (like mine approximates to), this is likely to only frustrate you!

Again, for those who have fairly straight-forward goals in "normal" contexts, the author's "Right Person – Right Approach" method purports to be able to make what would typically take months be accomplished in mere weeks; and Curtis is sufficiently confident in it that he gives his clients a *guarantee* of success, at least in achieving their micro objectives. But *those* are the people he's sitting in a room with, helping them achieve the "*clarity, control, and confidence*" to make this work. If you have that clarity going in, I'm sure this would be a awesome tool for achieving the goals you've already identified. However, if you're in the "don't know what I want to be when I grow up" boat (with me), there are no tools here to get to *"square one"* of this method, and the book is *not* a substitute for a coach in terms of distilling one's objectives from that grey matrix of vague preferences.

Anyway, this is brand new, so should certainly be on the shelves of the larger brick-and-mortar book vendors, and available to order at their smaller brethren. Amazon, however, has it at a generous 34% off of cover, and copies have already found their way into the new/used channels. As noted, I was very frustrated by this book, the "method" appears to be quite well conceived for those who know what they're shooting for, but it leaves the "big tent", "wide spectrum", "generalist" guys like me looking like road kill ... which may be just the way the world is these days, but it's damn depressing to have one's face ground in that while trying to connect with something that's promising better results.

Notes:

1. http://btripp-books.livejournal.com/99349.html
2-3. http://amzn.to/1qjzind

Monday, August 30, 2010[1]

How to be "remarkable" ...

So, a month or so back I indulged in one of those Barnes & Noble clearance sales in which I challenge myself to find 13 of the $1.99 books (to get up to free shipping at $25.00) that I'm interested enough to order. As I've noted, this is a good way to "randomize" my reading, because the things I'll decide on ordering are typically not in my regular reading rotation ... the current volume, however, is very much in line of what I've been plowing through recently, so I figured that it was worth noting that it semi-accidentally showed up in my to-be-read pile!

Part of me wonders how I'd missed reading any of Seth Godin's books over the past decade, but then I remember that, before starting in as The Job Stalker[2] last fall, I'd read only a mere *handful* of business or job-search books during the previous half-century ... so these would never have made it onto my radar before I found myself in an extended period of unemployment. Had I known that there were books like Free Prize Inside: How to Make a Purple Cow[3] out there, I might have reconsidered including the "business" genre in my reading. This is another very entertaining book by Mr. Godin, which also is a "call to action" for a vision of improved business/marketing.

Godin's publishing career has a lot of notable promotional concepts in play. The previous book to this (referenced in the sub-title) was "Purple Cow", and the book was sold inside a milk carton. Following up on that, the original edition of this book was packed in a *cereal box*, the book being the titular "free prize inside". Godin has recently shaken things up by announcing that from now on he's only going to produce e-books, and no more paper editions. Of course, if you're the best-selling author of more than a dozen titles, who has a wide and active Internet audience, this is a fairly easy decision to make (for most authors, this is pretty much a "don't try this at home" option at this point, however!).

What's this book about? Well, "free prize" is used metaphorically (although, obviously, in certain contexts it can be literal) as something that makes your product or service "remarkable" ...

> *The story is the product.*
>
> That's what he sells. That's what you sell. All dishwasher soap is basically the same. If the container tells a story, then it's part of the product. All cars are basically the same. If the styling tells a story, then it's part of the product.
>
> Please don't misunderstand me. If the product is lousy, or deceitful, or inadequate, or overpriced,

> that's a whole different story.
>
> But in our world of sameness, most of the time you're looking at parity of utility. So something has to happen.
>
> The way you make a Purple Cow is to be remarkable.
>
> The way you become remarkable is by creating a free prize. A bonus. Something extra, something worth paying for. A story that transcends the utility of the product and instead goes straight to the worldview of the user.

Godin spends the first half of the book making the case for this. From Amazon scrapping its entire ad budget to offer free shipping (gee, where have I heard about *that*?), to his own experience in getting his books onto the shelves in "unusual" packaging, he looks at how a successful "Purple Cow" can accelerate results far beyond what just throwing ad dollars at a project will, plus how to sell the idea to internal audiences whose first reaction would predictably be to derail the concept. The second half of the book takes a look at how you, me, anybody can come up with a "free prize" via his concept of "Edgecraft", *what's that?*, you ask ... *"Edgecraft is a methodical, measurable process that allows individuals and teams to inexorably identify the soft innovations that live on the edges of what already exists."* ... finding a "free prize" is not the same as product differentiation, it's making something that might be fairly generic *stand out*. One example he goes into is Budweiser, where a fairly average beer is "romanced" into a cultural icon ... the end user isn't ordering a Bud because it's *better*, he's ordering it to participate in some tribal identification. Of course, while A-B has spent a vast fortune to *create* that identity, some places do it by tweaking the experience (such as a Japanese haircut chain that is fast, cheap, and as automated as possible).

Also remarkable here is the notes section, which has page-number notes (so you have to keep checking) which range from a simple citation URL to a couple of pages of detail/digression on a subject, including a notable section on branding (where the Budweiser story comes in), with a particularly arch reference to *"the specialized form of hypnosis known as branding"* which has created an environment were *"quality has, in many cases, become entirely irrelevant"* ... some of the material back there is almost worth the cost of the book! Somewhat recursively, if the book was initially a "free prize inside" a cereal box, the free-standing edition also needed to carry a "free prize", and this is a free download of a 500-page e-book. The book in question is a resource directory of people and services that could help you produce your own "Purple Cow", unfortunately, this dates from 2004 (swell when this came out '04, perhaps less so six years down the road), so is likely to not be as useful as when first offered. Oh, and one other fairly amazing thing in here, there's a 2-page "condensed" version of the book in the last few pages ... Godin putting this in just in case you didn't have time to actually *read* the book, but your boss or client *had* and you wanted to at least be able to fake it ... *brilliant!*

Both the 2007 paperback edition (that I have) and the original 2004 paperback of Free Prize Inside[4] appear to still be available, so you'd likely be able to find one at a brick-and-mortar with a business section, however the *hardcover* of the 2004 edition is all over the new/used channels with numerous "very good" copies going for a penny (well, plus the $3.99 shipping), although Amazon has both the paperbacks for well under ten bucks. Anyway, this is a highly recommended read for anybody with an interest in marketing ... either products or one's "personal brand"!

Notes:

1. http://btripp-books.livejournal.com/99621.html
2. http://www.chicagonow.com/blogs/job-stalker/
3-4. http://amzn.to/1UWaqz9

Tuesday, August 31, 2010[1]

CAUTION: new age spewage ahead ...

Not that I've read them all, but James Redfield's books are always very aggravating for me ... they are so weak in some areas, barely even crafted in others, and yet have small gems of actual metaphysical knowledge buried in them. I was *shocked* when I read his *The Celestine Prophesy* to find a quite detailed description of a high-level "Incan shamanic" exercise right there in the same section that made me wonder if the guy had ever even set foot in Peru. Something similar is going on in The Secret of Shambhala: In Search of the Eleventh Insight[2].

Now, as regular readers know, I used to run a small metaphysical press, and Redfield is near legendary in that niche as a guy who built up his own little publishing empire on pretty much pure will and tireless promotion. He initially self-published *The Celestine Prophesy* and drove up and down the west coast selling copies, to whomever would buy them, from the trunk of his car. When you consider that only a tiny fraction of books ever sell even 10,000 copies (and that includes all the big publishers), it's amazing that he managed to sell 100,000 before "the big boys" noticed and picked up the book (which has now sold more than *20 million* copies world-wide). His example is always given as to what an author *can do* if they're totally dedicated to their book.

Anyway, The Secret of Shambhala[3] is the fourth book in that series, and sort of picks up mid-stream on the characters. This is a rare "novel" for me, as I've been avoiding fiction the past five or six years, and I'm wondering if the original book in the series was not presented as a novel when it came out. On one hand, this certainly lets the author off the hook for sounding like he's never been to the places he's writing about, but it also leaves one wondering about the writing, as there is nearly no "depth" to any of the characters (most appear to just be ways to advance the scene), and no "visual" aspect to much anything described (from his text, you'd think that Kathmandu and Lhasa looked like the more run-down areas of L.A.!). I've been to Kathmandu, and have seen many Tibetan temples, and you get *no* sense of the color, complexity, and fascination of these places here. And yet ...

The story here is that one of the protagonist's old associates suddenly needs him to be in Tibet, and that the protagonist, in a matter of days, is able (and willing) to turn around and fly to Kathmandu with little more than a couple of strange conversations. The plot involves him having to get to Shambhala (if you're not familiar with this, it's a legendary "hidden kingdom" in the mountains of Tibet) before the Chinese prevent him and his various contacts from finding their way there (really, the plot isn't much more involved than that, but it does include a lot of highly implausible activity). Along the way, the protagonist is tutored about "The Four Extensions" which deal with managing one's energy fields ... and *these* appear to be the whole purpose of the book. Two and half pages at the end of the book covers these four "energy workings", and I'm pretty sure the entire book is there just to "package them up" for mass consumption.

Again, I'm not the guy you want reviewing your fiction, as I don't have a lot of sympathy for it ... I don't read for "light entertainment" so it bothers me when there's almost nothing there, and there's very little "there" in this book, *except for* The Four Extensions. Even his big "plot twist" is telegraphed from the beginning of the book, and he wraps it up with a thick layer of treacly newage "things are changing for the good" blather (this came out in 1999 so a lot of the Kum-bay-yah "religious harmony" stuff sounds mighty non-visionary in a post 9/11 world). There is some *interesting* "technology" that the Shambhala folks have, which might or might not have a reality outside of the book, but, generally speaking, you can pretty much get everything of value here in those few pages which recap the Extensions.

Oddly, there was a section here about things that "call to you", and I must admit, I was "called" to pick this up at the OpenBooks[4] sale a few weeks back, and again "called" to shift this up to the top of my to-be-read mountain, so *maybe* this is stuff about energy work that I needed to read (I was reminded of a series of exercises that I'd begun from *another* book while reading this, so it might have been a prod in that direction), but it also reminded me why I don't generally read any fiction. Your mileage may vary.

The hardcover edition that I have appears to be out of print, but it is still available in the paperback (no doubt in any store with a New Age section) ... there are copies of the hardcover, however, in the Amazon new/used channels for as little as 1¢ (plus shipping) in "very good" condition, so that might be your best bet if you felt like getting this.

Notes:

1. http://btripp-books.livejournal.com/99998.html
2-3. http://amzn.to/1Q3glKv
4. http://open-books.org/

Tuesday, September 7, 2010[1]

Paranoid ...

This was one of those "pig in a poke" acquisitions from the Barnes & Noble on-line clearance sale (where I try to find 13 $1.99 books to get up to free shipping on the order), and it is as "odd" as any that have come my way via that channel. Ronald K. Siegel's Whispers: the Voices of Paranoia[2] is a rather strange book; it reads like fiction, but is based in the actual clinical work of its author. Dr. Siegel is "Associate Research Professor in the Department of Psychiatry and Bio-behavioral Science at UCLA", and is "frequently called upon as an expert in high-profile criminal cases". Most of the stories here hinge on this latter role, as the paranoia discussed has, generally speaking, expressed itself in lethal endgames. However, the former role is key as well, as much, if not all, of the paranoid episodes detailed are drug-induced, and his experience is both clinical *and personal* in this area.

I had to chuckle a number of times in reading this, reflecting on various psychiatrists that I encountered in my years of "metaphysical studies", as some of them seemed to have only gotten into that line of work *for the drugs*, and were frequently in possession of a wide array of psychoactive substances in their traveling kits. Obviously, if one is studying the mind, and subjective states *of* the mind, it can be argued that one can't really understand the subject without subjecting oneself to the chemicals which create "interesting" states ... this goes all the way back to Freud's cocaine use. This is most excessively illustrated here in one section where Siegel is "researching" the conditions that one subject was in during a multi-day stand-off where he shot his sister, watched his infant nephew die of dehydration, shot up the train car they were traveling in, and did a *vast* lot of coke ... which Siegel attempts to match, line for line!

While that is, perhaps, the most extreme of the cases outlined in the book, the dozen he discusses are *all* pretty bizarre, from the folks who are convinced there are tiny black bugs under their skin (and worms, and other stuff), which they gouge, scrape, burn, etc. to get rid of, to a guy who decides that he is God, but who is frustrated that the Doctor (who had been a stage magician in his youth) is able to produce more dramatic "miracles" than he can. In between, he interviews "Hitler's brain" (an Eliza-like computer program that a neo-Nazi tech wiz had obsessively developed with all the sayings and writings that he could amass from the mad dictator) ... works with a satellite scientist who had, largely based on a very strange movie, become convinced that a vast conspiracy (and dwarfs) were out to get him ... dissuades an old lady from her conviction that nanobots were installed in her teeth by her dentist, causing the title's "whispers" ... looks at the situation of a ballerina/hostess whose increasing cocaine use leads her to kill the object of her desires ... visions of bugs, and midgets, and assorted other drug-induced critters that leads one man to suicide, and another to killing his girlfriend's kid ... a chess prodigy who had "snapped" in Viet Nam, and was living out a progressively more macabre war game around him ... a gal who killed her daughter while in the midst of a religious fantasy fueled by a combination of drugs and preachy TV ... and a big-time drug dealer who was convinced that he was being stalked by (again) dwarfs.

All these are little trips down the rabbit hole ... from the full-on replicating of the train siege to the Hunter S. Thompson like "playing along with" the dealer's dwarf hunts, Siegel is himself caught up in each of these stories, to the extent that one has to wonder how "real" these tales are, and how "fictionalized" they may have become in the telling here. He is the author of a couple of other books (described as "highly regarded"), so I'm assuming that these are fairly close to reality, as strange (and sometimes implausible) they appear to be.

Whispers[3] does appear to still be in print, so you might be able to find it in your local book vendor's psychology section, but it's also out there in the new/used channels for under a quarter for either the hardcover or paperback editions. It's an unsettling, but fascinating read ... if the subject matter is of interest to you, it's certainly worth picking up!

Notes:

1. http://btripp-books.livejournal.com/100231.html

2-3. http://amzn.to/232Gnuc

Wednesday, September 8, 2010[1]

Bad, bad Bubba ...

It is something of a testament to the variety of my reading that this book emerged at the top of my "to be read" pile, not due to any inherent order, but for its *amusement* value. I am both a fan of Christopher Hitchens and a long-time despiser of the Clintons (causing much cognitive dissonance in my rooting for ~~Jiang Qing~~ ... ~~Hitlery~~ ... *the former First Lady* in the final months of the 2008 Democratic primaries) ... so, having a combination of Hitchens' acid analysis, and a *leftist* broadside on the Clintons, promised, if not much hilarity, at least a healthful heaping of *schadenfreude*. No One Left To Lie To: The Triangulations of William Jefferson Clinton[2] certainly did not *disappoint* on this level, although it wasn't the out-right trash-fest that some of my favorite books on the Clintons have been.

In fact, if there was a *bête noire* here, it's not Bubba, but the *author* of many of my favored Clinton texts, Dick Morris. It is evident here that Mr. Hitchens had a particular dislike of Mr. Morris, and this surfaces again and again in the course of this book, like he had been the little "devil" figure perched on the philandering POTUS' shoulder, whispering all the worst ideas into The First Ear. Now, I will admit that most of what I've known about Dick Morris' role in the Clinton political machine (both in Arkansas and DC) comes from his own books, in which, it is fair to assume, he would be unlikely to paint himself too much the villain. However, the level of despite that Hitchens harbored for him is rather remarkable, and came as quite a surprise.

This is not to say that Hitchens *excuses* the abuses of Bill Clinton because of what he saw as Morris' "evil influence", or even really suggests that Bubba wouldn't have been as venal without the "Morris factor". There was certainly enough vileness in the Clinton White House to go around, and the guy behind the big desk is where "the buck stops". Indeed, at one point, Hitchens notes: *"Clinton's private vileness meshed exactly with his brutal and opportunistic public style"* ... surely nothing more accusatory came from the pens of the likes of Gingrich, et al.

One thing to note, No One Left To Lie To[3] came out in 1999, and was half-written when the Impeachment was happening, so there is both an "immediacy" to those unfolding events, and a lack of a wider "historical context" of how those played out (although there are several very interesting "historical parallels" noted to assorted Clintonian assaults on ethics). The book walks through most of the better-known "abuses of power" of the administration, if in less damning detail than later books, from the selling of the Lincoln Bedroom, to the cozy relations with Chinese intelligence operatives, the flaunting of all fund-raising rules (frequently as flippantly "triangulated" as Clinton's infamous *"It depends on what the meaning of the word 'is' is."*), and his random attacks on foreign countries, timed only to deflect the media's attention from embarrassing events at home. Of course, to liberal Hitchens, the "worst" of Clinton appears to be his hijacking of the *Republican agenda*, in which he time and again created a cynical shadow policy of anything the other side might have wanted to enact. Or, as Hitchens more floridly puts it (in discussing Clinton's concern for "his place in history"): *"He will be remembered as the man who used the rhetoric of the New Democrat to undo the New Deal. He will also be remembered as a man who offered a groaning board of incentives for the rich and draconian admonitions to the poor."*

Hitchens despairs the near-universal blanket support (at the time, although the enabling "it's just about sex" parrot chorus is certainly still going strong) for Clinton among the left. His own writings about the abuses of the Clintons appear to have made him "persona non-grata" among many of his erstwhile friends and associates, some of whom would whisper in private that they felt that Clinton should have been Impeached, but for the various abuses of power and blatant disregard for the law, yet none of these would stand against the Clintons when it counted. Again, this book was written in the thick of the battle, and one gets the sense that Hitchens was feeling very isolated and a bit like "a voice in the wilderness" in his willingness to point out what should have been evident to all and sundry.

I wonder if, in the past decade, Hitchens has softened to Morris. After all, some of the most damning information about what happened in the Clinton White House has come from the many books that Morris wrote (including his "counter texts" to Bill and Hillary's much-ballyhooed memoirs). Would this be seen as a redemption, or just another form of despicability?

Anyway, I got the hardcover of this at the big OpenBooks[4] sale a few weeks ago, and it appears to be out of print in this edition (although "very good" used copies start as low as 1¢ via the Amazon new/used guys), but a later, expanded (and re-subtitled to include more about Mrs. Clinton), paperback edition does still seem to be in print. Needless to say, I really wish that a lot of those Liberals out there would sit down and read this, as it's coming from one of "their guys", and ask themselves why they were such suckers *{ahem}* for the Clinton regime. For the rest of us, well, it sure is a pleasant change to see *somebody* on the Left noticing what cretins they have managed to foist on the nation!

Notes:

1. http://btripp-books.livejournal.com/100462.html
2-3. http://amzn.to/1osGpsl
4. http://open-books.org/

Sunday, September 12, 2010[1]

Too many cooks ...

I had heard mention of The Twitter Job Search Guide: Find a Job and Advance Your Career in Just 15 Minutes a Day[2] via a Tweet by @HRMargo, congratulating one of its authors on its publication. I dug around a bit, looked at the promotional stuff about it, and contacted the publishers to *request* a review copy (kindly provided to me by the folks at Jist[3]), which I only rarely do. This is one of the reasons that I'm sorry that I'm not more enthusiastic about this than I am. This is a book that I should have *seriously* connected with, given that it is titularly about both the main thrust of my own job search, *and* most of what I write about over at the Tribune's *Chicago Now* blog, The Job Stalker[4]. However, I found it oddly irritating, for reasons that took me a while to sort out.

It would only be fair to say, as is often the case when I'm "reacting" to books this way, that much of the dissonance I felt with this no doubt comes from my "not being like the other kids on the block", and, *to my ear*, much of the advice ladled out here is oriented towards the same old "be a featureless zombie worker fitting a very narrowly-defined slot" that I encounter over and over in my job search reading. Obviously, on this point *"your mileage my vary"*. However, my core problem with the book is that it's quite a mishmosh of opinions, not *just* from the *three* named authors (which would be quite enough cooks hovering over this particular soup) Susan Britton Whitcomb, Chandlee Bryan, and Deb Dib, but *thirty-four* "chapter contributors" as well. Due to this cacophony of voices, the tone, focus, organization, and pacing of the book careen wildly from chapter to chapter.

I found it very strange that once the first section of the book discusses Twitter and social media in general, rather than moving to the section with the basic how-to on getting set up and using Twitter, a rather strident section called "Get Branded to Get Landed" comes in second, and only *then* do they address the actual use of Twitter. If I were a newbie looking at using Twitter as a job search tool, I'd be totally freaked out by this (as if one needed to jump through all those "personal branding" hoops in order to Tweet!), and I'd never have made it to section three. One gets the sense that the first three sections came from the named authors, and that some editorial infighting resulted in their strange order, after which the book opens into a torrent of almost random (albeit thematically arranged) material from the crowd of other folks involved.

Of course, the *upside* of having over three dozen contributors is that they bring a vast lot of information with them, however, the *downside* is that it's a daunting amount of advice/instruction/opinion to sort through. I've been on Twitter for over three years, and have been using it actively in my job search for more than a year, and *I* found this off-putting, so, as useful as this "firehose" of verbiage might be, drop for drop, I'm guessing a total Twitter newbie would find this very hard to deal with.

Given these caveats, while this plethora of info is hard enough to even list/discuss here, it is no doubt quite a useful *resource*, and I have something like a dozen bookmarks stuck in my copy, meaning there was a *lot* that I intended to go back to. Certainly if you are an individual in a *clearly defined* job search, with a focused list of what you wanted to do, and where you wanted to do it, you would be able to pick up this book and run with it, as *most* of the contributors here are very set on those sort of "square block in a square hole" situations (as evidenced by the frequent chastising of the reader about any variance from "on message" communications). Oddly, one of their contributors is quoted saying: *" Nobody is truly one-dimensional and most employers don't want an employee who is."*, in a section immediately preceding a chapter on "discretionary authenticity" which basically outlines the importance of not having *any* personality (or, at least, what I would recognize as personality) appearing in one's Tweets, which one is also coached to have be 75% about work (oddly, never defined in terms of one's *job search*) and only 25% about personal concerns!

But, hey, I'm in my *sixteenth month* "between jobs", so probably the dancing troupe of HR professionals and "Certified this" and "Certified that" folks who have penned this are *right* and I'm a moron for having problems with it. Obviously, *my* approach to the job search hasn't yielded any results that anybody would want to emulate, so I guess that should be a ringing endorsement for The Twitter Job Search Guide[5]!

As this has just come out, and is about a trendy topic, I'm pretty sure that you'll be able to find it at any book vendor with a job/business section. Amazon, of course, has it at a third off, so you might consider that. Again, to me, the authors make using Twitter in one's job search sound positively *terrifying*, but that's me, and I'm unemployed. If you're a square peg looking to find just the right square hole, this might be the ideal book for you.

Notes:

1. http://btripp-books.livejournal.com/100624.html
2. http://amzn.to/1ZWFQoj
3. http://www.jist.com/
4. http://jobstalker.info/
5. http://amzn.to/1ZWFQoj

Saturday, September 18, 2010[1]

English lit ...

This is one of those charming "Dover Thrift Editions", the little gems that I throw in when my on-line book (or other, this went in with a CD and a wireless adapter) order is a bit shy of the free-shipping "promised land". As I've noted previously in this space, I've taken advantage of these "economic add-ons" (this $1.00 book saved me $7.56 in shipping!) to plug in gaps that are still out there from my (otherwise excellent) liberal arts education.

While D.H. Lawrence is most famous (notorious) for his *Lady Chatterley's Lover*, he had a reasonably successful career as a writer in the period just before, during, and for many years after World War I. According to the editor's introductory essay: *Lawrence authored some of the twentieth century's greatest short stories, novels, essays, criticism, travel writing, and poetry. So powerful is his fiction that it overshadowed his poetry. A contemporary of Pound, Hardy, Eliot, and Yeats, his exuberance and intensity were unmatched by any of them.* The poems in <u>Snake and Other Poems</u>[2] are collected from four of his poetry collections, as well as a half dozen or so periodicals (the editor noted his regret of the absence of a few later poems, which are still under copyright). I was somewhat surprised, given the "theme" of the book leaning towards his "animal poems" to find how sexual many of these are, dealing obliquely with relationships between men and woman, or directly with marital interactions. The theme even finds its way into the animal poems, with much of the "Tortoise" material dealing with the mating activities, here's how "Tortoise Shout" concludes:

> Sex, which breaks us into voice, sets us calling
>   across the deeps, calling, calling for the complement,
> Singing, and calling, and singing again, being answered,
>   having found.

> Torn, to become whole again, after long seeking for what is lost,
> The same cry from the tortoise as from Christ, the Osiris-cry
>   of abandonment,
> That which is whole, torn asunder,
> That which is in part, finding its whole again throughout the universe.

Themes of sex, and death, and loss, and longing weave through these poems. They are old enough to seem from a different world (most have a rural setting), but there is a modern voice (and, strangely enough, some very modern phrasing in parts) within them. The sex here is not explicit, the frame shifting from voice to voice, be it man to woman, or age to age. The violence of the animal kingdom is more plain, be it the death of a rabbit, or the decline of a man. Here's the end of another poem, "And Oh – That the Man I Am Might Cease to Be –"

> *What is sleep?*
> *It goes over me, like a shadow over a hill,*
> *but it does not alter me, nor help me.*
> *And death would ache still, I am sure;*
> *it would be lambent, uneasy.*
> *I wish it would be completely dark everywhere,*
> *inside me, and out, heavily dark*
> *utterly.*

The volume is, as is usually the case with the Dover Thrift books, quite slim, just over 60 pages including title page, intro, etc., so this is hardly a encyclopedic look at Lawrence's poems, but it's an interesting exposure to his voice, which reached more infamous levels in other contexts. The odds of finding this in your local book vendor are also rather slim (the $1.00 cover price leaves little room for markup!), but it's in print so could be ordered, but these are best kept "at the ready" when you find yourself with an order to one of the on-line guys which hasn't quite made it to $25 and the free shipping.

Notes:

1. http://btripp-books.livejournal.com/101059.html
2. http://amzn.to/1RxKDKL

Sunday, September 19, 2010[1]

Notes on the Universe ...

I was very excited to "win" this book through the Library-Thing[2] "Early Reviewers" program, as there were only a few copies in play and a vast lot of folks requesting it. Given that popular physics books are one of my favored genres, I wasn't particularly *surprised*, just very pleased that the L.T.E.R. "Almighty Algorithm" saw fit to match my library with this title (and I felt "special" getting a pre-publication ARC paperback). I don't know what I was expecting from Stephen Hawking (whose *A Brief History of Time* has become a classic on the Science shelves), but The Grand Design[3], (at first blush, at least) oddly enough, wasn't it.

This is certainly a *different* book, looking at laws, and models, and what might or might not appear as "design" (and what that could suggest), and Hawking (with his co-author Leonard Mlodinow) walks the reader from the star-watchers of the ancient world, to the earliest stirrings of the scientific worldview in the Ionian culture, where the first concept of physical *laws* (as we would think of them today) were formulated. Once one has "laws" one can use these to model reality ... although the particular model one derives might be quite variant from the next guy's. An example is given of the world view of a goldfish in a round bowl ... were the fish equipped for philosophic contemplation, they would notice that everything beyond their bowl appeared to move along curved paths, and from these observations formulate laws which would allow for models of reality which would be, within their context, sufficiently predictive. The first part of the book continues looking at how the various different "threads" of reality evolved over the past couple of thousand years, up till the modern era.

The next section of the book looks at experiments and theories that have come to provide the basis of the modeling which is moving towards the "theory of everything" ... a vast lot of stuff is covered here, from the slit experiments which show the dual-nature of light (and other particles), and experiments which show what Einstein referred to "spooky action at a distance", time within Relativity, and on through Quantum ElectroDynamics, Feynman diagrams, Quantum ChromoDynamics, the structure of subatomic particles and the forces involved, to get to "M-theory" with multi-dimensional structures and alternative universes.

Once I got through this part, I realized what was bothering *me* about this book. I have read many volumes on these subjects, individually and collectively, and what was showing up here was a skimming (albeit quite informative) *overview* of all these things. Obviously, were one to hit this book *without* the background I bring to it, this would likely be a "down the rabbithole" experience of strange (but true) scientific thought. Somehow, I guess I was expecting, being that this is by *Stephen Hawking*, something that was going to amaze me, and instead it was more of a "CliffsNotes" on a dozen or so books that I'd already read.

Hawking spends most of the rest of the book trying to fit various cosmological data in with the structure of "M-theory" which he appears to favor as a framework for an over-all model for reality (although, oddly enough, he's not sure where the M term came from ... I'd always assumed it was the "membrane" of various "brane" models), which includes multiple universes, string theory, etc., etc., etc. Frankly, it seems to me that some of the "pulling together" here is a bit tenuous, almost as if Hawking was, faced with the continuing deterioration of his physical state, trying to *force* a unified theory out of the available bits and pieces of advanced work currently being done. Here's the closing paragraph of the book:

> *M-theory is the unified theory Einstein was hoping to find. The fact that we human beings – who are ourselves mere collections of fundamental particles of nature – have been able to come this close to an understanding of the laws governing us and our universe is a great triumph. But perhaps the true miracle is that abstract considerations of logic lead to a unique theory that predicts and describes a vast universe full of the amazing variety that we see. If the theory is confirmed by observation, it will be the successful conclusion of a search going back more than 3,000 years. We will have found the grand design.*

Of course, who am I to second-guess the likes of Hawking? I just felt that he gave a bit short-shrift to the multiverse theories and the related "Copenhagen interpretation" which suggests that *all* possible universes occur and that we're here simply because we couldn't exist in the vast majority of alternate universes (although he does certainly "go there", but somewhat in passing in discussing a wide range of cosmological factors, noting that, within M-theory *"there are probability amplitudes for perhaps as many as 10^{500} different internal spaces, each leading to different laws and values for the physical constants"*), *his* discussion of this "Anthropic principle" is fairly brief, and primarily serves as a pivot into discussing stellar chemistry.

Again, if one hasn't read a wide array of material on the cutting edges of physics, The Grand Design[4] is likely to be a "WOW!" experience for you. My disconnection with the book is due to there being very little "new" in here from what I've previously read (the experience was somewhat like that of reading a travel book about one's own city, interesting, but not necessarily eye-opening). However, taken on its own merits, it's an *amazing* book, especially given the sheer *volume* of discreet bits of scientific thought, historical as well as up-to-the-moment, crammed into a book that barely clocks in at 200 pages.

As this book is just out this month, all your local book vendors *should* have it (I'm writing this in a B&N Cafe, and there's a big display of the hardcover edition right up by the entrance!) but Amazon (at this writing) has it at a rather whopping 45% off, which is quite a deal (a few copies have surfaced in the "used" market, but at this point they're going for *more* than the new). I really did *like* this book, it was just that I was waiting form some "fabulous new thing" pay-off, which (given my interest in this area) it wasn't set-up to deliver. However, if you've not been paying attention to physics over the past decade or so, this will catch you up on quite a lot of what's been happening on the "cutting edge", as filtered through one of the great minds of the age!

Notes:

1. http://btripp-books.livejournal.com/101300.html
2. http://librarything.com/
3-4. http://amzn.to/232AOvH

Monday, September 20, 2010[1]

This is how you do it ...

Sometimes review copies arrive unannounced, sometimes I get queried about my interest, and sometimes I have to *beg* for a copy ... this is one of the latter cases. Not, of course, that the good folks at Wiley were being *stingy* with review copies, it's just that I'd followed the development of this book for a long time on Twitter, and I was feeling *much* put-off that I was reading Tweets about other people getting the book, enjoying the book, and reviewing the book, and I was still copy-less with my virtual face pressed up against the glass seeing what a swell book party was happening *without me*! Needless to say, I was *thrilled* when this finally came in.

Scott Stratten is one of those "Twitter guys" that one gets to know if one is serious about Social Media, as he walks the walk and talks the talk, and he'll even interact with you, despite having some 65,000 followers. His Twitter handle is @UnMarketing, and it was no great surprise that the book appeared as UnMarketing: Stop Marketing. Start Engaging[2] It has amused me to have been a bit of a "Twitter voyeur" for the genesis of a couple of really great social media books ... having been in the publishing field before, I was certainly familiar with the struggles that authors go though, but it's been quite interesting to see that play out on my computer screen.

As you have no doubt guessed at this point, I think that UnMarketing[3] is *awesome* (or, as its author would have it: "awesomesauce"). This is as much by a "digital native" as a book (with "Twitter" in its title) I recently reviewed in this space *was not* ... although Scott does describe his initial tepid response to Twitter, and his rather over-the-top "one last try" that eventually turned him into a major social media advocate. Tellingly, this book does not have "Twitter" in its title (even though the first half of the book "takes place" within that 140-character zone), because it's really about approaches of engagement and the things that work, the things that don't, and the companies (and people) who "get it", and those that don't.

The book opens with one of Stratten's most repeated stories, of being out at BlogWorld in Las Vegas and encountering a member of the maintenance staff at the brand-new Wynn casino/hotel whose eager, authentic, and individualized "customer service" (to somebody just wandering in to take a look) made a difference in the perception of the "brand" that millions of dollars of ads, press releases, imprinted tchotchkes, etc. could not. There are several stories here of times that Scott went "undercover" to see how various businesses were at "customer experience", and much of what he reports is pretty grim, although the text is somewhat "bookended" by another story of somebody "doing it right", with his experience on one of these ventures with the staff of a Lush soap store.

In between these there is a wealth of tales of folks who are at various points on that "getting it" spectrum. As noted, about the first half of the book is mainly Twitter, while the rest of the book moves out into more general settings, from tips on how to improve web experiences, to various ways of delivering information, to assorted business settings, etc., all seasoned with Scott's own experiences and painful mistakes (and some of those are *doozies*). He discusses newsletters, mailing lists, web hosting, audio and video conferences, live conferences, trade shows, etc., and shows what's good, what's bad, and what is, frankly, ridiculous. The "skewering" of various unquestioned "best practices" begins with the book's back cover[4] which reduces standard publishers' quote-mongering down to their essential absurdities.

UnMarketing[5] is, in its primary focus, a book for businesses, but in the age of the "personal brand" most of what Stratten preaches to the business audience is equally applicable to the individual, at least as far as presenting themselves authentically within their specific personal contexts. If you have an interest (as I do) in the nitty-gritty of Social Media, this is also a great resource for things that Scott has found (frequently via painful trial-and-error) to work best, from programs to services to systems, and the vast majority of the bookmarks I dropped in here were pointing to things like this that I'm planning on getting back to.

The book is a quick read, enhanced by generally short chapters (most in the 3-6 page range) focused on specific topics, with only one going beyond 10 pages, the 26-page section on Viral Marketing (which I'm guessing was re-purposed for the book from some previously e-formatted material). Throughout Scott uses his self-depreciating humor to balance the "sacred cow goring" barbs aimed at those who are "doing it wrong". At one point Scott asks to know if you had "WOW!" moments in reading the book, and while I can't say that, I can report that in several instances I was Laughing Out Loud over his descriptions of various quirks in himself and others. If there was one thing that stood out in this book over all the other Social Media books I've read, it's his very specific descriptions of how *he* screwed up things over the years, with detailed instructions on how to avoid his mistakes. This make the book feel more like "hanging out with a Social Media mentor" than attending a seminar on the subject, which is quite notable in its uniqueness.

As this just officially came out a couple of weeks back, you should be able to find it all over the place (at least at book stores that carry business/marketing/internet books), but, at this writing, Amazon has it for 34% off of cover, and that's even cheaper than what it's going for via the new/used vendors. If you have an interest in social media, customer service, business, personal branding, or figuring out ways that folks can simply "not be jerks"; this is a book you'll like; it's witty, direct, and speaks from experience.

Notes:
1. http://btripp-books.livejournal.com/101421.html
2-3. http://amzn.to/1YmPH65
4. http://www.un-marketing.com/back.jpg
5. http://amzn.to/1YmPH65

Tuesday, September 21, 2010

A perfect match ...

Sometimes the Universe just brings you what you need. I picked up a copy of Roddy Lumsden's Vitamin Q: A Temple of Trivia Lists and Curious Words via one of the $1.99 clearance sales on the BN.com site, and, frankly, wondered when or even if I'd ever get around to reading it. You see, this is a big thick book full of *lists*, sure, they're *amusing* lists, even *informative* lists, but it's essentially reading a reference book, which (as one can imagine) leaves something to be desired as a project. I imagine that this is both intended and ends up as "toilet reading", as most of the material in this ranges from a half a page to five pages, perfect time-fillers for when one is otherwise occupied, as it were.

So, why did I *need* this right now? No, I haven't contracted dysentery or anything along those lines ... but *my computer* is quite ill at the moment, with something which causes it to freeze up at totally random times, requiring a hard re-boot. These re-boots, while irritating (especially before I got in the habit of neurotically saving whatever I was working on!), only took from 3-5 minutes to get from swearing and pushing the power button to being back into what I'd been doing before I'd been so rudely interrupted. These little gaps in my schedule (and there were something like *a hundred* of them over the course of the past few days), are what were *perfect* for reading this book, as I was able to get in 3-4 pages of reading for every re-boot cycle!

The author of this is a very rare bird, as he *claims* to make a living off of being a poet. That is, in this day and age, somewhat akin to being a Sealing Wax Magnate. I see from Wikipedia, that he also *teaches* poetry, so there's some salary in play there that's not dependent on readings and chapbook sales. He is also a Scotsman, and a non-trivial percentage of the material in here is focused on the Scottish linguistic heritage ... which, if this isn't your particular thing (mine neither), is rather tedious. A lot of the stuff here, too, hangs on knowledge of and interest in British TV and music, with much of that eliciting the predictable glassy-eyed stare from your typical Yank (myself included).

However, at least half the book is quite interesting, with some sections (more wordy than simple lists) being evidently well researched, and some pieces being what could be quite effective seeds for a stand-up routine (*"Fourteen Words That Mean The Opposite Of How They Sound"* most stood out on this point). However, it's hard to even get through a list of 70+ butterfly/moth names, or several dozen horse maladies! This all originates with the "Vitamin Q" website the author started "out of boredom" a decade or so back, and the 360 or so pages here appear to be a "data dump" of the materials backlogged there.

Again, had I not been having computer problems (and I'm *hoping* that as of tomorrow, I'll be back on a different machine!), I don't know if I'd ever have gotten around to reading Vitamin Q[3], and it was just *perfect* to distract me over those otherwise-maddening re-boot cycles. It does appear that this is out of print currently, but the Amazon new/used guys have "like new" copies for as little a one cent (plus the $3.99 shipping, of course), so it is out there if things like *"Personal names which have a different meaning in old Scots"* (90 of 'em), or *"Forty things which people have claimed to be responsible for 'the worst smell'"* pique your curiosity enough to want to obtain a copy!

Notes:

1. http://btripp-books.livejournal.com/101761.html
2-3. http://amzn.to/1Vnag28

Sunday, October 3, 2010[1]

Social media for social change ...

As regular readers of this space know, I am not "like all the other kids on the block" and sometimes I run into stuff that just doesn't mesh with me at all, and, unfortunately, The Dragonfly Effect: Quick, Effective, and Powerful Ways To Use Social Media to Drive Social Change[2] seems to be in this category. There isn't anything in particular that set me off on this, but reading it was something like one of those old silent films where two train cars are on different, but adjacent, tracks and nothing that the riders do manage to get them in sync.

Perhaps this is another "too many cooks spoiling the soup" effort, as I have found that recent "team written" books I've read to never settle into a groove for me. The nominal authors of this are a husband-and-wife team, Jennifer Aaker (a professor of marketing at Stanford University's Graduate School of Business), and Andy Smith (a marketing consultant), however, a *third* author, Carlye Adler, was involved enough to make it onto the title page. If that wasn't enough, there is a *12-page section* of acknowledgments (oddly stuck in between the notes and the index) in the back, called "The Dragonfly Ecosystem" in which they detail what they admit to being "a massively collaborative effort", it is here that one gets the sense that the reason that much of the book seems so *random* is that it is, to a non-trivial extent, a collection of Aaker's students' projects.

Frankly, there was never an "AHA!" moment where the concept of "The Dragonfly Effect" clicked. Rather, there was a prevailing sense that the authors wanted to do something cute (and copyrightable) as a riff of the famed chaos-science theory of the "Butterfly Effect" and then worked *backwards* from that to pull together an approach that both fit some dragonfly-esque imagery and was able to include social media and be applicable to "social change". Now, admittedly, despite my involvement with various non-profits over the years, I am *not* a "social change" (as the authors understand it, at least) kind of guy. I would be interested in hearing how my numerous friends "in that business" react to this, as maybe it's akin to a book about *accounting* or something, and I'm just not in its *audience*. In any case, *to me*, this very much read like a book where the authors had pulled together assorted shiny things, stuck them in a box, kept adding stuff until it looked full, and then dumped it out on table to organize into something that fit the pattern they were looking for. There are useful bits and pieces in here, there are handy approaches to things, but (again, to me) this never seemed to gel into something coherent.

Anyway, here are the items that seem to stand out ... there are "four key skills": Focus, Grab Attention, Engage, and Take Action (oh, and each of these are "wings" on the dragonfly) ... there are the concepts of "stickiness", "ripple effects", and "emotional contagion" ... there are sub-systems like "HATCH" goals for focusing (Humanistic, Actionable, Testable, Clarity, and Happiness), the "PUVV" (?) "design principles" for grabbing attention (Personal, Unexpected, Visual, and Visceral), the "four design principles of Engagement", "TEAM" (Tell a story, Empathize, be Authentic, and Match the media), and those for enabling others to take action: "EFTO" (Easy, Fun, Tailored, Open) … and grids like "how to ask" which takes dimensions of "emotional intensity" and "social distance" and blocks out approaches. An interesting feature of the book are the several "flow charts" included to walk folks through some of the sub-sub-systems, and there are various other "walk through" sidebars with pretty solid utility (the "tell a story" section, for instance). The entire "system", however, manages to fit on a single page (p.162), and put out in that format it does look a bit thin. There is also "coaching" on how to get into and use social media, but it really is not integral to the process itself.

Given my near-exclusive reading of *non-fiction* books, I rarely have to make this sort of warning, but "SPOILERS AHEAD". There are a number of "case studies" in here looking at how assorted people had used social media to achieve various aims. I found it *bizarre* that most of the stories involved terminally ill patients who, while achieving their organizational/functional goals, *all died* without having benefit of the efforts. The "group" efforts profiled are, generally speaking, great successes (such as Kiva), but it was grim going from case to case where the success is tempered with ultimate failures for the individuals! The book also focuses more on the Obama campaign than I feel is justified (sure, they made effective use of new media, but had 99% of the MSM working as enthusiastic unpaid shills for the campaign, which sort of skews the results), but what do you expect from a college professor from California?

Again, it *may* "just be me" here, but the caveats discussed above are not illusory, and (as noted), I'd be interested to hear what a "social change" person felt about this as a "system". There is good stuff in here, but as Churchill said of a pudding, it appears to "lack a theme" to make it a satisfactory whole. Obviously, the plethora of voices involved might be to blame for this, or my suspicions of this being "reverse engineered" from observations of class projects, but it's a box full of stuff of assorted value, and I guess it depends on how that plays out to you to how worthwhile you'll find this.

This officially just came out last week, so it should be available via the brick & mortars, but Amazon has it for more than a third off of cover, and the new/used guys have "new" copies already at well under half of the cover price. This book and I never were connecting, but "your mileage may vary" … I didn't *hate* the book, but have a hard time recommending it unless it sounds like something you've been looking for! Your best bet might be to delve into their web site http://www.dragonflyeffect.com and see how this sits with you.

Notes:
1. http://btripp-books.livejournal.com/101967.html
2. http://amzn.to/1Vn9jXG

Sunday, October 17, 2010[1]

But not really ...

This was a book obtained from the LibraryThing[2] "Early Reviewers" program. As frequent readers of my reviews here may have a sense, the books that come to me via that channel are frequently not what I would have wished them to be (at least judging from the brief synopsis provided on the announcement listing), and this, unfortunately, falls in that zone as well. Frankly, Graham E. Fuller's A World Without Islam[3] diverges significantly from its description. The book I was *expecting* was one based on a "thought experiment" of an alternative history in which Islam had never flourished, spread, and stamped its mark on wide swaths of the world, the book I ended up reading was not this at all, instead being a chain of "excuses" for Islam "not being at fault" for assorted conflicts across continents and centuries.

As I've previously noted in this space, I very rarely go digging into other reviews posted on the net prior to my writing my own, but this was one of those cases where I was wondering if I was "missing something" in this, and went to see what others had said about it. There was a certain dichotomy, of course (many thought this was *brilliant*), but I was amused at those who suggested that this project was "paid for by CAIR", as it does seem to be exclusively intended to paint Islam as the "aggrieved party" in almost any historical situation where it might have otherwise been at least suspected to have been at fault.

Of course, my next question was "who is this Graham Fuller guy?", as the easy *assumption* from the tone of the book would be that he was some mush-headed left-wing college professor looking to "stick it to the Man" with this sort of tome. Much to my surprise, however, not only is Fuller not in academia, he's not even a PhD (although he does have a Masters from Harvard in Russian), which led me momentarily to consider him to simply be a pro-Islamic crackpot. Upon more research, I was further amazed (given the tone of the book) that he spent 27 years in the State Department and *the CIA* (serving as Station Chief in Kabul!), and had even been the vice-chair of the National Intelligence Council before leaving government work for a no-doubt better-paying role at the RAND Corporation.

Needless to say, this created more confusion for me, as this guy is unlikely to be a raving "fifth column" agitator, a tenured Marxist drone, or even somebody simply grossly misinformed. How then to explain the book? It is structured in three sections, "Heresy and Power", "Meeting at the Civilizational Borders of Islam", and "The Place of Islam in the Modern World", spinning out the history of Islam within the world. On this level, as a history, it's quite a useful and interesting book, but rather than looking at "what might have been" scenarios of what the world would have been like *without*

Islam, again and again the focus is on how things would have been "just as conflicted" in the numerous regions and times given geopolitical and cultural stresses existing beyond Islam *per se* ... sort of like saying that if the same people who are currently Islamic found themselves in the same situations they'd be as much a problem for the West as they are, but they just wouldn't be Islamic (which isn't really the same thing as looking at a world minus that particular monotheism).

The first section looks at Islam as something like a Judeo-Christian heresy, not unlike many other heresies of the time, and how this fit in with the early evolution of Christianity. It then looks at Rome and Byzantium, and the conflicts and cultures represented by these, with Islam's eventual conquering of the Eastern empire and the balance developed between the Orthodox Church and Islam. Next the Crusades are discussed (painting Islam in a much gentler light than the Crusaders), and tracks the interactions of Islam with Christianity up into the Protestant Reformation.

The second section looks at Islam's engagement with various other cultural entities. This is probably the most informative part of the book, as much of the material here was completely new to me, and I'm *assuming* that Fuller isn't fudging on the facts to bring his biases to the fore. There is a long look at Russia, and how Orthodoxy was attempted to be put forward as "the Third Rome", and how this influenced Byzantium and the various Asian regions where both Russia and Islam had influence (all those "stans" late of the Soviet Union). The notable cultural interface of Islam with India is covered, as is the somewhat surprising Islamic incursion into China, and in a chapter titled "Muslims in the West: Loyal Citizens or Fifth Column?" Fuller takes a look at the frequently uncomfortable fit of Islam in cultures that are either primarily secular or nominally Christian.

The final section looks at the modern issues with Islam, and the role that Colonialism, Nationalism, and various revolutionary movements have had in that interface. The subject of terrorism comes up here, but in such an excuse-laden form as to be hardly recognizable, as it is framed in a way that the belief that the West is to blame for everything, and anything done to lessen the prestige, power, or prosperity of the West is *justifiable* in the cultural milieu in which Islam operates. The final chapter is looking forward at future scenarios. Although from the tone of the book, one might think that Fuller would be advocating at that point for submission to Sharia Law, he rather suggests that *"Washington should act as if Islam did not exist in formulating its policies in the Middle East."*, a suggestion that would seem to be doomed to failure when dealing with people for whom *their religion* is central to their cultural identity! But, hey, I'm not a RAND Corp. consultant, so what do I know?

Anyway, the distance between the A World Without Islam[4]'s description and its reality felt to be something of a "bait and switch", and the dissonance of those poles were a constant irritation while reading this. As noted above, as a *history* there is much to commend this, but it would have helped to have had it be presented as what it is (perhaps titled *Islam Is So Much Cooler Than You Think It Is* or somesuch). This is fairly new (it just came out in August), so if you're interested in picking up a copy, your best bet might be through Amazon, who has it at 34% off at the moment (the new/used guys don't have it for much less at this point), but there's still a decent chance that your local brick-and-mortar might have copies as well. Again, while I found parts of this informative, I felt is was pushing an agenda beyond the nominal purpose of the book. Needless to say, "your mileage may vary", especially coming to it forewarned.

Notes:

1. http://btripp-books.livejournal.com/102325.html
2. http://btripp-books.com/
3-4. http://amzn.to/1RGFm0j

Tuesday, October 19, 2010[1]

A useful little book ...

Yes, I was a Comparative Religion major in college, and have read extensively in the area for the past 30 years, so one would think that a book like Laura S. Smith's The Illustrated Timeline of Religion: A Crash Course in Words & Pictures[2] was a bit basic for me to be delving into. However, this was one of those semi- "pig in a poke" titles from one of those Barnes & Nobel clearance sales that I'd ordered pretty much sight-unseen due to it being available for a whopping $1.99 ... as I've noted previously, these sales have an interesting side-effect of getting books in front of me that I would have been somewhat unlikely to have picked up were I actually "book shopping" rather than "trying to find 13 books to get over $25 for free shipping"!

As one might guess from the title, this is hardly an in-depth survey on any aspect of the subject matter, rather, in a bit over 100 pages, this looks at religious manifestations, figures, movements, etc., from prehistoric ages right on through its publication in 2005 (the current Pope's election is the penultimate entry here). The book is formatted in a horizontal alignment, and (keeping with the "timeline" theme) a line goes across most of the pages (there are some section-starting pages with more extensive essays on progressive "ages"), with small dated paragraphs pointing to their appropriate position within the flow of time. The pages are all at least *half* taken up by pictures, so the amount of text is at a minimum, however, due to the vastness of the subjects (and the lack of any particular *narrative* to move things along), this is not exactly a quick read ... think of it more like a stack of many hundreds of index cards, and you'll get the feeling of what the reading experience is like. The text is also color-coded to reflect where the individual person, cult, construction, etc., was, with six colors representing the populated continents, and Australia.

Again, I have read *extensively* on Religion and there was very little in here which I hadn't at least heard of (with the exception of the remarkable temple of Borobudur in Java, which I have since Googled the heck out of), but I was *amazed* at how my *perceptions* of when various things happened in relation to others were off, sometimes by embarrassingly large spans of time. This comes, I suppose, from studying things within their own little bubble, and if there wasn't some major "time anchoring" event (like the Spaniards destroying the Aztec and Incan cultures) to put them into context, they were free to float off to whatever corner of my temporal grid that they seemed to fit.

It is fascinating to realize how old the Vedas or the great Chinese sages are, especially when compared to Buddhism, and more especially Vajrayana (the Gelugpa sect being scarcely 600 years old, at least on the physical plane), how far into the "A.D." zone the Mishna and Talmud appeared, and the fact that Mormonism is slightly *older* than Shinto! Perhaps it is from my getting older, but at this point in my life, I carry around *fifty years* worth of memories, and (when I'm not asking the opinion of my knees) I generally feel like a young man, so it is amazing to me that the Spanish conquest of the great American cultures in Mexico and Peru are only ten or so "sets" of memories ago (which, if I hold to the illusion of youth, would imply that it's simply a flash within pan-historical time).

While this might not be a "light read", I suspect that I will make frequent use of it as a reference for a quick check of when what happened in relationship to when other things happened, and so find it *highly* valuable, and a delightful surprise. It certainly is an *interesting* read, even for those not so into the subject matter, as the level of illustration is quite remarkable, and a bit like taking a nice little tour through the ages!

Staying on the theme of "one would think", given that I bought this on a *clearance* sale, one would think that one would be safe in the assumption that The Illustrated Timeline of Religion[3] was out of print or otherwise unavailable, but *both* Amazon and BN.com have it, the latter at a discount, and the former having new/used vendors with "very good" copies going for as little as three bucks and change. Cover price on this is only $12.95, so it's pretty reasonable even if you ended up picking a copy up at your local book retailer. Again, I wasn't expecting to learn much from this, and was quite pleasantly surprised to have come to have many things either clarified or added to my data banks! If you have any interest in the history of religion, this should prove to be a quite enlightening little book to have around for reference.

Notes:

1. http://btripp-books.livejournal.com/102608.html

2-3. http://amzn.to/238ORMS

Monday, October 25, 2010[1]

Like a cat needs a self-help book ...

OK, If I keep reviewing these, somebody out there is going to accuse me of being a "crazy cat ~~lady~~ guy", but the good folks at Ten Speed Press keep sending them and I keep finding them amusing, and so you get to read me bloviating about them. Actually, it's probably not fair to group in Dena Harris' Who Moved My Mouse?: A Self-Help Book for Cats (Who Don't Need Any Help)[2] with my previously-reviewed Careers for Your Cat[3] as they *are* by different authors, with different "hooks", but it is somewhat inevitable, as they both *look* so similar, featuring the whimsical art of Ann Boyajian (whose contribution made it to the cover credits on the previous book, but she ends up listed below "Mr. Nom-Noms" on the title page here).

Whereas the "Careers" book spoofed the genre of Myers-Briggs career guides, Who Moved My Mouse?[4] takes on an entire shelf-full of self-help books, one by one. Obviously, the joke here works best when one is familiar with the "source material" being re-imaged into a cat-centric universe (uh, as if there *was* another type), as I found the spoofs on the ones I had read being far more amusing that those on ones that I'd only heard of.

The book starts off with "A Cat's Conversations With God", which I assume to be spun off of the (unread by me) *Conversations With God* books, then moves into what appears to be a generic "*Purr*sonality Profile" (I couldn't identify a specific book this was imitating), and then into "How To Win Friends And Influence Dog People", no doubt following the non-Dog version by Dale Carnegie. Next it moves to the title chapter, "Who Moved My Mouse?: An Amazing Path to Declare Revenge on Those Who Dare Disturb What Is Yours", obviously paralleling *Who Moved My Cheese?: An Amazing Way to Deal with Change in Your Work and in Your Life*, and then to "Don't Sweat the Small Stuff ... But Feel Free to Freak Out Over Anything That Moves Suddenly or Without Warning" which echoes *Don't Sweat the Small Stuff--and it's all small stuff*, and on to "Nice Cats Don't Get the Corner Litter Box" which certainly owes a good deal to *Nice Girls Don't Get the Corner Office*. Stephen R. Covey's *The 7 Habits of Highly Effective People* transforms into "The 7 Habits of Highly Effective Cats", Don Miguel Ruiz' *The Four Agreements* become "The Fur Agreements" (and, interestingly, this is the only source book specifically credited with inspiration for a chapter here), and *The Worst-Case Scenario Survival Handbook* (which appears to deal with things like escaping from quicksand or performing a do-it-yourself tracheotomy) becomes "A Cat's Worst-Case Scenario Survival Handbook", with pointers on avoiding baths and vacuum cleaners. A "bonus chapter" on *The Secret* closes things out, but this is a mere 2 sentences long.

At one point a Chicago comedy troupe had an unofficial slogan: *"the drunker you are, the funnier we are"*, and I'm reminded of that when thinking about this book ... the *more familiar* the reader is with the "source material" the funnier the Cat-version takes on it will be. While this would be an amusing "kitty humor" book to somebody who had never wandered down the "business strategy" or "self-help" aisle of their local bookstore, it could well be a "gut-buster" for those who were both well versed in these genres, and can-opening adjuncts of the feline species. I, myself, am in the middle here, cohabiting with cats and having dabbled in the books in question, and I'm sure I found this far more amusing than some would, but far less so than others.

In any case, <u>Who Moved My Mouse?</u>[5] is a short, easy read, with a predictable (if variable) humor pay-off, so should be something that anybody would enjoy. This only officially came out last week, so it is very likely to be available at your local brick-and-mortar book monger, but both Amazon and BN.com have it on discount for under $10. This would be appreciated in general by "cat people", but is likely to most amusing to folks who are big into the books spoofed in it!

Notes:

1. http://btripp-books.livejournal.com/102835.html
2. http://amzn.to/1W3dh8J
3. http://btripp-books.livejournal.com/97257.html
4-5. http://amzn.to/1W3dh8J

Friday, October 29, 2010[1]

Not that strange ...

This is a book that I "won" back in June via the Library-Thing[2] "early reviewers" program, but did not receive the review copy until just this past week. Obviously, a book that came out in April, featured in June, and delivered in October, has lost a whole lot of the "early", but I did push this up to the top of the "what I'm reading" pile to get this out as soon as possible.

I'm not surprised that Michelle Souliere's Strange Maine: True Tales from the Pine Tree State[3] was featured by LibraryThing, as she resides (and operates a bookstore) in the same town, Portland, ME, that is home to the L.T. Home office, and I'm assuming that she's friends with them (although, I must admit that I had to dig a bit to find her LT profile, as she's not flagged with the "author button", and I've even got that!). She has been writing a blog for the past five years, also called "Strange Maine", and producing a print version as well. I guess coming up with a book was the next logical step.

While I rather enjoyed reading Strange Maine[4], I do have to note that the primary "take-away" that I had from it was *"is that all?"*, as the five chapters here (each covering a different sort of "strangeness") fill up exactly 100 pages, many of which are taken up by photos, illustrations, and extensive citations of verse. One would think that five years of blogging on the subject would have provided a bit more "meat" than what ends up between the covers here.

The book begins with "The Witch's Grave and Other Marked Monuments" which really only addresses *two* specific cases, although presented within a discussion of the various cemeteries in Portland, and civic cases surrounding these. The author does a substantial bit of investigation on the history of one of these, and then presents a bit of a present-time "ghost story" on another. Next is "Crime on the Coast, and Elsewhere" which discusses three notorious murders, again with a good deal of research involved (and at least one nod to Steven King), although the 3.5 pages of melodramatic verse from the mid-1800's commemorating one of these seems to be "overkill". The book then moves to "Places that Go Bump in the Night", a look at some supposedly spooky places ... although two of them (both decommissioned military facilities) appear to be more "spooky" due to being home to psychic fairs and mystical festivals than anything inherent to the locales ... the third tale in this section is simply a ghost story experienced by a friend of hers, who had sent it in. Fourth comes "What Monsters Roam in the Maine Woods?", which features a half-dozen or so "strange" animal tales ranging from an early version of Oberon Zell's "unicorn", to Emu farms, and assorted werewolf-related bits (much of this section is no doubt courtesy the author's bookstore sharing space with the International Cryptozoology Museum). Finally, there's "Oddities and Ephemera" which looks a quirky collections, including the aforementioned museum.

This is a reasonably engaging read, albeit a very short one (I managed to get through this in three 45-minute bus rides), with material that varies from quirky to really horrific (I really *didn't* need to read one of those murder stories). I think the book would have benefited from a map of the state, indicating where the various things were or had happened, and a bit more context about the history of the state (the stories jump around between centuries quite a bit).

Obviously, if you have an interest in what is "strange" in Maine, Strange Maine[5] is the book for you, but for most folks its recommendation sits more with it being engaging while being "odd", and a quick easy read. As noted, this came out earlier this year, so it may have slipped out of the bookstores to some extent by now, but both Amazon BN.com have it at a discount, so you can get it on-line.

Notes:

1. http://btripp-books.livejournal.com/103054.html
2. http://btripp-books.com/
3-5. http://amzn.to/1Vn33iO

Monday, November 1, 2010[1]

Don't judge this book by its cover ...

This is one of those books that arrived unannounced from a publisher (in this case Ten Speed Press), which *probably* would have done better with a query call or e-mail up front to put the book in context. Of course, having been penning *The Job Stalker*[2] blog (over on the Chicago Tribune's "ChicagoNow" site) for a year now (and featuring interviews with authors to go along with these reviews), I get a fairly steady flow of books about jobs, careers, and assorted related subjects. When Pam Lassiter's The New Job Security, Revised: The 5 Best Strategies for Taking Control of Your Career[3] came in, I glanced at it, flipped through it, checked out its chapter headings, and tossed it over in the "maybe sometime" stack. There was *nothing* in a cursory examination of this book which would have suggested to me that it was anything of interest to somebody enmired in a job search, appearing rather to be a "strategy" book for, well, "Taking Control of Your Career", implying to me, at least, that it was targeted to those lucky folks *who HAD careers* to "take control of" and *not* us pitiful job seekers. I even sent a somewhat "testy" e-mail to the publicist involved (perhaps in response to a follow-up e-mail query), indicating that a book dealing with ways to provide "job security" in one's career had somewhat minimal applicability to me or the readers of *The Job Stalker*. I was rather chastened when she replied that this was *indeed* a book with rather significant utility for the job seeker, and suggested that I start by checking out the middle section, "Stop Looking For Jobs".

Having now read The New Job Security[4] I can tell you that it can be a useful book for somebody "in transition", but I fear that unless one has somebody waving it under your nose and saying "LOOK HERE!" it is highly unlikely to be picked up off the bookstore shelf by somebody searching for tools to apply to their job search, which is unfortunate. The "revised" part of this is that Lassiter has updated her 2002 original version of the book to reflect the realities of our current disastrous economy. I have not seen the previous edition, but I *suspect* that it was much more targeted for executives who were job-shifting their way up the corporate ladder. However, she appears to be making use of the various tools and conceptualizations of *that* book here to such an extent (within a rather new economic reality) that she probably felt that she *couldn't* simply package those things up in new wrappings and market it as a different book (and I certainly respect that), but in doing so (and again, this is simply my *guess* as to how this new version came about) much of the former structure (and implied orientation) was maintained, leading to the confusion that I was having about it!

Anyway, the book is in 7 parts, the "5 Best Strategies" with an introductory and a closing chapter. To cut to the chase, as it were, here are the "strategies" involved:

Strategy #1: Send Clear Signals
Strategy #2: Market for Mutual Benefit
Strategy #3: Stop Looking for Jobs
Strategy #4: Build Sustainable Networks
Strategy #5: Negotiate in Round Rooms

Can you see how I didn't "get" this as a job-transition book? Much of the thrust here (as implied in #3) is to "create situations" rather than go out looking for "jobs", and Lassiter walks the reader through various steps, exercises, and "homework assignments" along the way (with some worksheets for these available at the TheNewJobSecurity.com web site).

The over-all impression I have of this is that the author has attempted to distill the sort of "career management consulting" that she does professionally into a comprehensive "manual" that individuals can use on their own. As these things go, I found this *far* less "nagging" than many similar books, and I believe that if one were to dedicate oneself to actually *working through* what she presents here, one would likely to show good results. From my own experience with the job search, I do not have the faith in the sort of networking that is presented here actually happening (which is a key element in the mix), but I'm not discounting that another person in a different situation might be able to make that work. One caveat, however ... most of the focus here is on people looking for six-figure upper management positions ... this may come from her affiliation with the ExecuNet organization, which is one of "those sites" that make you pay to access information on jobs, with the promise that they're pre-screened high-salary listings (which anybody familiar with my *The Job Stalker* scribblings know I have *significant* issues with) ... although certainly some of the tools here are generally applicable.

One thing that particularly recommends itself is a conceptualization called "the marketing circle" where the job seeker's needs are on one side, and the employer's needs are on the other. This is a handy way to keep one's focus on *filling needs* for the employer, rather that looking at (or communicating) the needs that you have.

Again, I don't know the thrust of the previous edition, but I really think this book would have benefited being "repackaged" into something that spoke more directly to the present-day job seeker. The new revision just came out last month, so it should be available in the brick-and-mortars, but Amazon has it at about a third off. I'd be careful with ordering a used copy, however, as the previous version appears to *still be in print* (how odd!), so unless you were very specific about the book you were ordering (I'm assuming they have different ISBNs), you might end up with something very different. Again, this is very good for what it is, but it's very hard to get to the point where one *knows* what that is!

Notes:
1. http://btripp-books.livejournal.com/103386.html
2. http://jobstalker.info/
3-4. http://amzn.to/1N3LVI4

Saturday, November 6, 2010[1]

Isn't that convenient ...

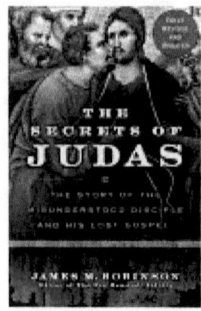

Sometimes it's a good thing having this wide-ranging background. I can certainly understand how somebody coming to this book from a "DaVinci Code" mind-set might find it remarkably disappointing, but being that I was a subscriber to *Biblical Archaeology Review* back in college this was reasonably interesting to me, on its own merits. James M. Robinson's The Secrets of Judas: The Story of the Misunderstood Disciple and His Lost Gospel[2] was one of those books featured in the last Barnes & Nobel on-line clearance sale for $1.99, so I picked it up with fairly limited details on the book. This is certainly being *marketed* with the Dan Brown crowd at least in mind, but it could hardly be more different from the assorted other books pitching "secrets" of a Biblical bent.

The author is an expert in Coptic documents from the first few centuries C.E., and did a good deal of work on the famed Gnostic collection, The Nag Hammadi Library. While some experts in the field of ancient literature have gone "off the deep end" from time to time (the name Sitchin comes to mind), this is not Robinson's course at all. Rather, this book is *primarily* about the "secrets" of the ancient document trade, the in-fighting, the smuggling, the lies and financial deals that lurk behind most of these resources coming to light. Robinson first encountered the materials comprising *The Gospel of Judas* through sources of somewhat questionable provenance in Geneva in 1983, and spends the first half of the book tracing the wanderings of these papyrus sheets (which he had declined to purchase) over the decades leading to their publication via a National Geographic project in 2006. Through this he rails against the closed system of exclusive access that seems to wrap around these ancient discoveries, leading to unreasonably long cycles of selected publication by anointed researchers (whose financial and professional interests are in play) while shutting out the vast majority of the field. This happened notoriously with the Dead Sea Scrolls, and the Nag Hammadi material, and the archaeological community had *tried* to set up regulations that would prevent this from happening, but the *Gospel of Judas* was similarly swallowed up by its representatives and erstwhile caretakers.

From reading *Biblical Archaeology Review* (which itself was often close to the center of some of these controversies) back in the day, and being quite familiar with much of the Coptic Gnostic material published over the past 30 years, I found the various plots, schemes, conspiracies, and other complications both interesting and, sadly, unsurprising. To those looking for power plays with shadowy Vatican figures, this would be *very* dry, however. The first half of the book traces the Judas material from its likely discovery (and historical context) on through the "blockbuster" publication Easter 2006.

The second part of the book is an analysis of the figure of Judas Iscariot, from several different perspectives. Separate chapters are given to "The Judas of the New Testament", "The Historical Judas", and "The Gnostic Judas", each looking at how this figure was framed, used, and integrated with various thematic, philosophical, and theological contexts. There are certainly *echoes* here of other books (several of which I've read) which take, to various extents, the somewhat Gnostic stance that Judas was "just following orders", being "in on" the symbolic necessities of Jesus' execution, but it's pretty clear that Robinson doesn't have a particular axe to grind here, although it's also reasonably sure that he's not much of a Bible thumper.

The final section of the book *discusses* the actual text of *The Gospel of Judas*, while not actually reproducing any of it (which is, I'm sure, due to copyright issues on the existing English translations of it, and on-going *access* issues to the Coptic originals preventing the author from offering up his own version). This again could prove to be a major disappointment to readers who were expecting to at least have *that* pay-off at the end of the book, but was only a slight issue for me, given the rest of the thrust of the book.

Oddly, compared to many of my reviews, I have to say that I enjoyed reading The Secrets of Judas[3] *far* more than I'd anticipate the vast majority of people who might be tempted to pick this up would (this reflected by the paltry 2.5-star rating this has on Amazon). If you disengage this from the "religious sensationalism" genre and drop it into the "academic/archaeological/religion research conflicts" genre, it makes perfect sense, and is quite a full and satisfying presentation of the material! Unfortunately, I'm guessing that fans of the latter are a vanishingly small demographic, so Harper has been having to peddle this with at least the "look and feel" of something that it really isn't.

As I've been discovering of late, having a book go out for $1.99 via a BN.com clearance does *not* mean that it's out of print. Both B&N and Amazon have it in stock (at a minor discount), and I'm guessing that copies might even be out in the brick and mortar book vendors who stock a decent-sized Religion aisle. However, the new/used guys are all over this, and "like new" copies of the hardcover, and *new* copies of the paperback can be had for a penny (plus, of course $3.99 shipping), so that would certainly be your best bet for picking this up. Again, unless you have an interest in the messy and somewhat *louche* world of the ancient text market, this might not hold your interest particularly well, but if that's "your thing", it's a great read.

Notes:

1. http://btripp-books.livejournal.com/103655.html
2-3. http://amzn.to/1REZmQR

Saturday, November 13, 2010[1]

The Heart of America ...

I've had a bit of a run of "good luck" in LibraryThing.com's "Early Reviewer program, having been matched up with review copies of 10 books over the past 13 months. As I pretty much only read non-fiction, the selection of titles that I might request is somewhat limited (out of the hundred or so books offered each month), but I find it interesting what is deemed (by "the Almighty Algorithm") suitable for my library, as it has varied quite a bit of late, especially considering that by "pure chance" the odds would run only 3-4% for "winning" one of these. This is the long way about to note that Robert Spector's The Mom & Pop Store: True Stories from the Heart of America[2] came to be in my "to be read" pile via this program, rather than being something that I specifically picked up.

Those who have been reading my main blog over the past decade will know that I come from an entrepreneurial background, and, while I've not operated in a retail environment since a high-school pharmacy stocking job, the stories in this book certainly have a deep resonance with me. The author is the son of a butcher from Perth Amboy, New Jersey; his grand-father being a Jewish immigrant from the Ukraine who arrived here in 1910, his family only able to join him *a decade later*. Like many subsequent generations of early immigrants, Spector did not care for the meat business, and went off to college and became a writer and speaker of some significant repute (see http://robertspector.com), but the memories were there, and in his 60's he made something of a pilgrimage, not to the physical sites of his youth, but to the "family business" culture which permeated it.

The first section of the book is about his family, their environment, and their business, much of it being a window into a quite different era of food production and distribution (while *his* family was most insistent on the best quality and the fairest dealings, there was quite an eye-opening story of another vendor in the market who sold "honey" which was cooked up at home out of sugar water and some caramel coloring!).

The second section of the book looks at the independent merchant, from its roots in ancient history, on through the modern era. Each point is illustrated with a story of a different small business operation, from delis, to bodegas, to carpet companies, ice cream shops, hardware stores, restaurants, and even a Japanese tea merchant. Spector traveled the world to speak to these dozens of "mom and pop" operators and get down their stories. Some of these are tales of survival, a few are of substantial successes, all of them speak of grit, determination and passion.

The last section is about how small businesses like these become an integral part of the communities in which they operate. Here the author returns to previous subjects, and looks at new situations such as small business trying to restore a sense of normalcy in their neighborhoods in the wake of Hurricane Katrina. He also returns the narrative to a personal level and takes a look at "mom and pop" businesses he knows in his current home in the Seattle area. These have a bit different tone, as he's doing some degree of "hometown bragging", but using that as a specific case of what can be generalized to any area. In this section he also "takes off the gloves" to some extent to stand up for the entrepreneurial sector. This particularly stood out to me:

> *If there's one thing officials of local and state governments enjoy more than giving incentives to big companies, it's hassling small businesses with lots of rules and regulations. Clearly, these elected officials and bureaucrats have never run a business. Too often, city, county, state, and federal taxing entities spend their time trying to squeeze money out of the most vulnerable contributing taxpayers: mom & pop stores. And if they're not after the money, they are trying to find ways to control commerce in the form of licenses. According to an editorial in the Wall Street Journal, more than 20 percent of the U.S. workforce is required to get a permit to do their jobs – as compared to a mere 4.5 percent in the 1950s.*

As a child of entrepreneurs, the spouse of an entrepreneur, and a one-time entrepreneur myself, the stories and underlying messages in The Mom & Pop Store[3] spoke deeply to me, and even inspired me to at least *fantasize* about businesses that I might begin (albeit not today, I'm too deep into this unemployment vortex to not be looking for the stability of a paycheck). If you have small businesses in your family, you will most certainly find similar points of resonance in here, and all others should probably read this just for the perspective it gives on this often-ignored (although substantial) segment of our economy.

While this is not *new* new (the hardcover came out last year), the paperback edition is, and should be available out there via your local "mom & pop" book vendor (or, if none of those have survived by you, the big chain stores). Both Amazon and BN.com have it at a discount, and the new/used guys have "like new" copies for as little as a couple of bucks (plus, of course, the $3.99 shipping), so this can be had for a very reasonable price. Again, because of my background, this had a significant appeal to me, and I'm hoping that this will be something that everybody would consider picking up.

Notes:

1. http://btripp-books.livejournal.com/103830.html
2-3. http://amzn.to/1RUOLR0

Sunday, November 21, 2010[1]

Write ... right ...

This was another book that showed up in my mailbox, courtesy of the good folks at Ten Speed Press, without a query or any notice ... *surprise!* Now, obviously, I'm a "book guy" and am, due to my on-going economic struggles, always happy to get books at substantial discounts, or, in the case of review copies, free. I do, however, from time-to-time get books that I am pretty much *just not interested in reading* (which makes me feel very guilty for having been sent them), and at first, I thought this was one of *those*. However, circumstances coalesced where this had, for purely "mechanical" reasons (being set up in fairly discreet chunks of limited length), suggested itself for filling in time while I was dealing with "computer issues", and so I was at least a significant ways into this by the time my computer problems miraculously resolved themselves.

What I discovered is that Be a Brilliant Business Writer: Write Well, Write Fast, and Whip the Competition[2] is a *very funny* book, or at least funny for the sort of book it is. This *is*, after all, something of "a manual of style", so lacks any *narrative* to draw the reader along. And, while there *is* a certain development as one moves through it, the book does not really "build" to any great pay-off, so this was certainly one of those "disciplined reads" rather than something that I was aching to block out time to get back to!

Again, this is a book about *Business* writing, and the author team of Jane Curry and Diana Young are certainly taking much of their own advice in how the book is laid out, as each of the 21 chapters begins with a bit of set-up discussion about the subject of that chapter, then a list of the specific points that are going to be covered, and then it walks through sections corresponding to those points. Frankly, it took me a while to "get this" (I can be dense sometimes), but what might have been perceived as a certain "choppiness" made sense once that structure became clear. Curry and Young have an editorial consultancy[3] (based in the Chicago area) which works with corporations to improve the quality of their communications. I feel safe in the assumption that Be a Brilliant Business Writer[4] is a product of converting their seminar and coaching materials into a longer-form book.

There are quips and jabs sprinkled all through here, but I was about a quarter of the way through the book when it struck me how *intentional* this was, when in the "If You Want To Write With The Right Tone" chapter, in the first of three sections, "Apply The Two Critical Tenets Of Good Tone", I discovered that:

> *The two most critical tenets of good tone are:*
> • *Your lips are your best friends. If you wouldn't say it, don't write it. {...}*

> • Nobody likes attorneys, or at least not the way they convolute language. {...}

Yep, those are the 2 tenets! There are many other bits of "coaching" through here which are similarly shooting for levity (e.g. *"Because you are not a sociopath and don't want to inflict pain on your readers, you want to write clearly and concisely."*!), as well as barbs directed to those composing pieces *not* adhering to these guidelines (a good deal of the book is given over to "before" and "after" variations of documents, and one of the things that makes this somewhat of a slog to read is *getting past* those "before" versions).

The book flows through three focuses, the first third or so are the basics (and, are the "best part"), dealing with writing and communication in general, with clear instructions as to how to avoid the numerous pitfalls targeted here. The second third or so is much more dense, but that's because it's dealing with things like "write for senior management", "share technical information", "write procedures that people can actually follow", "write financial documents", "PowerPoint presentations", "executive summaries" and "sales letters" ... none of which is exactly Oprah's Book Club material. The final third looks at various bits and pieces, like thank you notes, resumes and cover letters, coaching on when to use or not use e-mail, and how to move from "academic" to "business" writing styles.

There are certainly a number of corporate/institutional "sacred cows" being gored in Be a Brilliant Business Writer[5], but over-all the advice appears to be very good (even in the sections that made my eyes glaze over), and this would certainly be a help to anybody whose writing skills are under-developed and is looking for a way to better themselves. This came out in early October, so should certainly be available in your local brick-and-mortar book shop that features business titles, but the on-line guys currently have it for 25% off of the very reasonable cover price, so it's in the ballpark of throwing it together with something else to get up to the free shipping promised land. This isn't exactly relaxing beach or fire-side reading, but if you're looking to punch up your business communications, it's no doubt a good investment.

Notes:

1. http://btripp-books.livejournal.com/103993.html
2. http://amzn.to/1W1C5hg
3. http://www.curryyoung.com/
4-5. http://amzn.to/1W1C5hg

Saturday, November 27, 2010[1]

A really remarkable book ...

As regular readers know, I typically start off these reviews with a little bit about how I came to be reading the particular volume under consideration. This one had a somewhat odd appearance in my to-be-read pile, having been obtained in response to a post that author Seth Godin had made in his blog to the effect that he was once again opening up membership in a closed Ning site to anybody who had read either Tribes or Linchpin. As I had not previously encountered either, I took the opportunity to pick up a copy of the former via Amazon's new/used guys, and reasonably quickly got it into the reading mix. Unfortunately, it was not quick *enough*, as by the time I'd finished this and went to go sign up, the offer had already expired.

However, Godin's Tribes: We Need You To Lead Us[2] was hardly a waste of time and money on my part. Over the past year I've become somewhat of a fan of Seth's, and catch up with his frequent (if generally rather brief) blog postings via my Twitter stream on a daily basis. This is (from those I've read) a much more "inspirational" sort of book, as it looks at belonging, leading, and how groups (tribes) form around various points of attraction. Tribes[3] is not a large book (in either dimensions or, at 151 pages, length), but it is a rather enthusiastic examination on its subject. Organized in a hundred or so sections (each from a few sentences to a few pages long), most of this looks at people who did something to change the game, redefine the discussion, or emerge as leader. The concepts of "leading" and "tribe" are important here, and while Godin doesn't do a carved-in-stone defining of how he means these terms to be taken, he leave many clues: *"The skeptical among us look a the idea of leadership and we hesitate. We hesitate because it feels like something we need to be ordained to do. That without authority, we can't lead. That big organizations reserve leadership for the CEO, not for us."* ... this coming from a section where one person, initially with one PowerPoint presentation, instigated sweeping changes *in the Pentagon* (does an organization get more bureaucratic and formalized?). The concept of "tribe" is everything one would typically associate with the word, but spread out to include corporations, religions, fans of bands, etc.: *"Tribes ... aren't about stuff. They're about connection."*, a Tribe is a crowd with a leader and internal communication.

Concepts of fear (which is the most common block to being a leader), and curiosity come into play ... leaders are typically quite curious, always willing to ask the questions that lead to change ... and if you ask *enough* questions, you get to be a *heretic*! As one might expect, the subject of heretics works its way around to faith and religion:

> *Faith leads to hope, and it overcomes fear. ... Faith is critical to all innovation. Without faith, it's suicidal to be a leader, to act like a heretic.*
>
> *Religion, on the other hand, represents a strict set of rules that our fellow humans have overlaid on top of our faith. Religion supports the status quo and encourages us to fit in, not to stand out."*

What Godin looks at here aren't just the "big R" Religions, but "religions" of companies, countries, educational specialties, neighborhoods, etc. ... another great line here is *"If religion comprises rules you follow, faith is demonstrated by the actions you take."*

Another couple of images spun out in Tribes[4] are those of "the Balloon Factory" (and its unicorn) and "Sheepwalking" (the activity of *"people who have been raised to be obedient"* when given *"brain-dead jobs and enough fear to keep them in line"*). "The balloon factory is all about the status quo. And leaders change the status quo." Godin talks about encountering "sheepwalkers" everywhere, even where you might expect them to not be (such as Google!). The "sheepwalkers" are not the people you need in your organization (or tribe): *"When you hire amazing people and give them freedom, they do amazing stuff. And the sheepwalkers and their bosses watch and shake their heads, certain that this ... is way too risky."* Perhaps opposite of these folks are the "positive deviants": *"Managers stamp out deviants. That's what they do. ... Great leaders embrace deviants by searching for them and catching them doing something right."*

As you can tell, I found all this quite engaging, and was very enthused with the whole concept, up until the point where Godin challenges his readers to establish their own "Micromovement" (with six Principles and a five point action plan) using the Internet for leverage ... that's when the Fear hit and parts of my psyche went scurrying for cover, which is why I haven't slogged into Point 1 - "Publish a Manifesto"! I guess one thing's missing: *"Every tribe leader I've ever met shares one thing: the decision to lead"* ... I'm sill working on that.

Anyway, I heartily recommend Tribes[5] to all and sundry ... it's quite a manifesto in its own right for being something other than that "normal" out there which is constantly crushing out all things of real value. This came out a couple of years back, but it's sufficiently popular that I'm pretty sure you'd have no problem finding it at your local brick-and-mortar book vendor. It's a bit pricey for it's size, but if you take it to heart, it's certainly worth the cover price (although I did get mine via the used channels). If I had the resources, I'd have bought a half a dozen copies to give to associates to read ... it really is a remarkable book!

Notes:
1. http://btripp-books.livejournal.com/104230.html
2-5. http://amzn.to/1ODUEjm

QR code links

to the

on-line reviews:

The Five-Minute Miracle
by
Tara Springett

Peace Kills: America's Fun New Imperialism
by
P.J. O'Rourke

Entangled Minds:
Extrasensory Experiences in a Quantum Reality
by
Dean Radin

How to Self-Destruct:
Making the Least of What's Left of Your Career
by
Jason Seiden

The Union of Their Dreams:
Power, Hope, and Struggle
in Cesar Chavez's Farm Worker Movement
by
Miriam Pawel

How to Thrive in Changing Times:
Simple Tools to Create True Health, Wealth, Peace,
and Joy for Yourself and the Earth
by
Sandra Ingerman

A Chicago Tavern:
A Goat, a Curse, and the American Dream
by
Rick Kogan

Me 2.0: Build a Powerful Brand
to Achieve Career Success
by
Dan Schawbel

1001 Things It Means to Be a Boomer Now:
(Well, It Is Time to Grow Up)
by
Harry H. Harrison Jr.

Crush It!
Why Now Is The Time To Cash In On Your Passion
by
Gary Vaynerchuk

Super-Freakonomics:
Global Cooling, Patriotic Prostitutes, and
Why Suicide Bombers Should Buy Life Insurance
by
Steven D. Levitt & Stephen J. Dubner

Songs of Milarepa
by
Milarepa

Trust Agents: Using the Web to Build Influence,
Improve Reputation, and Earn Trust
by
Chris Brogan & Julien Smith

The Last Three Minutes
by
Paul Davies

CrazyBusy: Overstretched, Overbooked, and About
to Snap! Strategies for Coping in a World Gone ADD
by
Edward M. Hallowell M.D.

Get Seen:
Online Video Secrets to Building Your Business
by
Steve Garfield

In the Dark Places of Wisdom
by
Peter Kingsley

Social Media 101:
Tactics and Tips to Develop Your Business Online
by
Chris Brogan

Viral Loop: From Facebook to Twitter,
How Today's Smartest Businesses Grow Themselves
by
Adam L. Penenberg

Fired!: Tales of the Canned, Canceled,
Downsized, and Dismissed
by
Annabelle Gurwitch

Utopia
by
Sir Thomas More

The Writer's Voice
by
A. Alvarez

Ethical Ambition: Living a Life of Meaning and Worth
by
Derrick Bell

Use Your Head to Get Your Foot in the Door:
Job Secrets No One Else Will Tell You
by
Harvey Mackay

Cro-Magnon: How the Ice Age
Gave Birth to the First Modern Humans
by
Brian Fagan

Social Media Metrics: How to Measure
and Optimize your Marketing Investment
by
Jim Sterne

On Guerrilla Warfare
by
Mao Tse-tung

Get The Job You Want Even When No One's Hiring
by
Ford R. Myers

The 4-Hour Workweek:
Escape 9-5, Live Anywhere, and Join the New Rich
by
Timothy Ferriss

10 Make-or-Break Career Moments:
Navigate, Negotiate, and Communicate for Success
by
Casey Hawley

Traveler's Guide to The Ancient World
The Roman Empire: Rome and its Environs in the Year 300 CE
by Dr. Ray Laurence
Ancient Greece: Athens and its Environs in the Year 415 BCE
by Eric Chaline
Ancient Egypt: Thebes and the Nile Valley in the Year 1200 BCE
by Charlotte Booth

Effective Immediately: How to Fit In, Stand Out,
and Move Up at Your First Real Job
by
Emily Bennington & Skip Lineberg

The Next Wave of Technologies:
Opportunities in Chaos
by
Phil Simon

Permission Marketing: Turning Strangers Into Friends
And Friends Into Customers
by
Seth Godin

Riding Toward Everywhere
by
William T. Vollmann

Twitterville: How Businesses Can Thrive
in the New Global Neighborhoods
by
Shel Israel

The Magic of Thinking Big
by
David J. Schwartz

Collider:
The Search for the World's Smallest Particles
by
Paul Halpern

The Maya
by
Michael D. Coe

KaChing:
How to Run an Online Business that Pays and Pays
by
Joel Comm

Cash In A Flash: Fast Money in Slow Times
by
Mark Victor Hansen & Robert G. Allen

Rewired: Understanding the iGeneration
and the Way They Learn
by
Larry D. Rosen, Ph.D

Careers For Your Cat
by
Ann Dziemianowicz & Ann Boyajian

What Your Body Says (And How to Master the
Message): Inspire, Influence, Build Trust, and Create
Lasting Business Relationships
by
Sharon Sayler

Angkor: Temples of Cambodia's Kings
by
Dawn F. Rooney

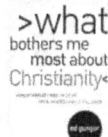

What Bothers Me Most about Christianity:
Honest Reflections from an
Open-Minded Christ Follower
by
Ed Gungor

Rework
by
Jason Fried, David Heinemeier Hansson
& Mike Rohde

Glenn Beck's Common Sense:
The Case Against an Out-of-Control Government,
Inspired by Thomas Paine
by
Glenn Beck

On Seeing: Things Seen, Unseen, and Obscene
by
F. Gonzalez-Crussi

The Art of Business Seduction:
A 30-Day Plan to Get Noticed,
Get Promoted, and Get Ahead
by
Mark Jeffries

Mutant Message Down Under
by
Marlo Morgan

Well Connected: An Unconventional Approach
to Building Genuine, Effective Business Relationships
by
Gordon S. Curtis

Free Prize Inside: How to Make a Purple Cow
by
Seth Godin

The Secret of Shambhala:
In Search of the Eleventh Insight
by
James Redfield

Whispers: the Voices of Paranoia
by
Ronald K. Siegel

No One Left To Lie To:
The Triangulations of William Jefferson Clinton
by
Christopher Hitchens

The Twitter Job Search Guide:
Find a Job and Advance Your Career
in Just 15 Minutes a Day
by
Susan Britton Whitcomb, Chandlee Bryan, & Deb Dib

Snake and Other Poems
by
D.H. Lawrence

The Grand Design
by
Stephen Hawking & Leonard Mlodinow

UnMarketing: Stop Marketing. Start Engaging.
by
Scott Stratten

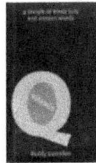

Vitamin Q:
A Temple of Trivia Lists and Curious Words
by
Roddy Lumsden

The Dragonfly Effect: Quick, Effective, and Powerful
Ways To Use Social Media to Drive Social Change
by
Jennifer Aaker, Andy Smith & Carlye Adler

A World Without Islam
by
Graham E. Fuller

The Illustrated Timeline of Religion:
A Crash Course in Words & Pictures
by
Laura S. Smith

Who Moved My Mouse?:
A Self-Help Book for Cats (Who Don't Need Any Help)
by
Dena Harris & Ann Boyajian

Strange Maine:
True Tales from the Pine Tree State
by
Michelle Souliere

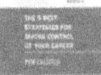

The New Job Security, Revised:
The 5 Best Strategies
for Taking Control of Your Career
by
Pam Lassiter

The Secrets of Judas:
The Story of the Misunderstood Disciple
and His Lost Gospel
by
James M. Robinson

The Mom & Pop Store:
True Stories from the Heart of America
by
Robert Spector

Be a Brilliant Business Writer:
Write Well, Write Fast, and Whip the Competition
by
Jane Curry & Diana Young

Tribes: We Need You To Lead Us
by
Seth Godin

CONTENTS - ALPHABETICAL BY AUTHOR

Jennifer Aaker, Andy Smith, Carlye Adler   page 135
The Dragonfly Effect

A. Alvarez   page 46
The Writer's Voice

Glenn Beck   page 103
Glenn Beck's Common Sense

Derrick Bell   page 49
Ethical Ambition

Emily Bennington, Skip Lineberg   page 69
Effective Immediately

Charlotte Booth   page 66
Traveler's Guide to The Ancient World –
Ancient Egypt: Thebes and the Nile Valley in the Year 1200 BCE

Chris Brogan   page 38
Social Media 101

Chris Brogan, Julien Smith   page 26
Trust Agents

Eric Chaline   page 66
Traveler's Guide to The Ancient World –
Ancient Greece: Athens and its Environs in the Year 415 BCE

Michael D. Coe   page 84
The Maya

Joel Comm   page 86
KaChing

Jane Curry, Diana Young   page 152
Be a Brilliant Business Writer

Gordon S. Curtis   page 112
Well Connected

Paul Davies   page 29
The Last Three Minutes

Ann Dziemianowicz, Ann Boyajian *Careers For Your Cat*	page	92
Brian Fagan *Cro-Magnon*	page	53
Timothy Ferriss *The 4-Hour Workweek*	page	61
Jason Fried, David Heinemeier Hansson, Mike Rohde *Rework*	page	101
Graham E. Fuller *A World Without Islam*	page	137
Steve Garfield *Get Seen*	page	33
Seth Godin *Free Prize Inside*	page	115
Seth Godin *Permission Marketing*	page	73
Seth Godin *Tribes*	page	154
F. Gonzalez-Crussi *On Seeing*	page	106
Ed Gungor *What Bothers Me Most about Christianity*	page	98
Annabelle Gurwitch *Fired!*	page	42
Edward M. Hallowell M.D. *CrazyBusy*	page	31
Paul Halpern *Collider*	page	81
Mark Victor Hansen, Robert G. Allen *Cash In A Flash*	page	88
Dena Harris *Who Moved My Mouse?*	page	142

Harry H. Harrison Jr. *1001 Things It Means to Be a Boomer Now*	page	18
Stephen Hawking, Leonard Mlodinow *The Grand Design*	page	128
Casey Hawley *10 Make-or-Break Career Moments*	page	64
Christopher Hitchens *No One Left To Lie To*	page	122
Sandra Ingerman *How to Thrive in Changing Times*	page	11
Shel Israel *Twitterville*	page	77
Mark Jeffries *The Art of Business Seduction*	page	108
Peter Kingsley *In the Dark Places of Wisdom*	page	35
Rick Kogan *A Chicago Tavern*	page	13
Pam Lassiter *The New Job Security, Revised*	page	146
Dr. Ray Laurence *Traveler's Guide to The Ancient World – The Roman Empire: Rome and its Environs in the Year 300 CE*	page	66
D.H. Lawrence *Snake and Other Poems*	page	126
Steven D. Levitt, Stephen J. Dubner *SuperFreakonomics*	page	22
Roddy Lumsden *Vitamin Q*	page	133
Harvey Mackay *Use Your Head to Get Your Foot in the Door*	page	51
Milarepa *Songs of Milarepa*	page	24

Sir Thomas More *Utopia*	page	44
Marlo Morgan *Mutant Message Down Under*	page	110
Ford R. Myers *Get The Job You Want Even When No One's Hiring*	page	59
P.J. O'Rourke *Peace Kills*	page	3
Miriam Pawel *The Union of Their Dreams*	page	9
Adam L. Penenberg *Viral Loop*	page	40
Dean Radin Ph.D. *Entangled Minds*	page	5
James Redfield *The Secret of Shambhala*	page	118
James M. Robinson *The Secrets of Judas*	page	148
Dawn F. Rooney, Michael Freeman *Angkor*	page	96
Larry D. Rosen, Ph.D. *Rewired*	page	90
Sharon Sayler *What Your Body Says (And How to Master the Message*	page	94
Dan Schawbel *Me 2.0*	page	15
David J. Schwartz *The Magic of Thinking Big*	page	79
Jason Seiden *How to Self-Destruct*	page	7
Ronald K. Siegel *Whispers*	page	120

Phil Simon		page	71
	The Next Wave of Technologies		
Laura S. Smith		page	140
	The Illustrated Timeline of Religion		
Michelle Souliere		page	144
	Strange Maine		
Robert Spector		page	150
	The Mom & Pop Store		
Tara Springett		page	1
	The Five-Minute Miracle		
Jim Sterne		page	55
	Social Media Metrics		
Scott Stratten		page	131
	UnMarketing		
Mao Tse-tung		page	57
	On Guerrilla Warfare		
Gary Vaynerchuk		page	20
	Crush It!		
William T. Vollmann		page	75
	Riding Toward Everywhere		
Susan Britton Whitcomb, Chandlee Bryan, Deb Dib		page	124
	The Twitter Job Search Guide		

CONTENTS - ALPHABETICAL BY TITLE

10 Make-or-Break Career Moments
Casey Hawley — page 64

1001 Things It Means to Be a Boomer Now
Harry H. Harrison Jr. — page 18

The 4-Hour Workweek
Timothy Ferriss — page 61

Angkor
Dawn F. Rooney, Michael Freeman — page 96

The Art of Business Seduction
Mark Jeffries — page 108

Be a Brilliant Business Writer
Jane Curry, Diana Young — page 152

Careers For Your Cat
Ann Dziemianowicz, Ann Boyajian — page 92

Cash In A Flash
Mark Victor Hansen, Robert G. Allen — page 88

A Chicago Tavern
Rick Kogan — page 13

Collider
Paul Halpern — page 81

CrazyBusy
Edward M. Hallowell M.D. — page 31

Cro-Magnon
Brian Fagan — page 53

Crush It
Gary Vaynerchuk — page 20

The Dragonfly Effect
Jennifer Aaker, Andy Smith, Carlye Adler — page 135

Effective Immediately
Emily Bennington, Skip Lineberg — page 69

Dean Radin Ph.D.	Entangled Minds	page 5
Derrick Bell	Ethical Ambition	page 49
Annabelle Gurwitch	Fired!	page 42
Tara Springett	The Five-Minute Miracle	page 1
Seth Godin	Free Prize Inside	page 115
Steve Garfield	Get Seen	page 33
Ford R. Myers	Get The Job You Want Even When No One's Hiring	page 59
Glenn Beck	Glenn Beck's Common Sense	page 103
Stephen Hawking, Leonard Mlodinow	The Grand Design	page 128
Jason Seiden	How to Self-Destruct	page 7
Sandra Ingerman	How to Thrive in Changing Times	page 11
Laura S. Smith	The Illustrated Timeline of Religion	page 140
Peter Kingsley	In the Dark Places of Wisdom	page 35
JoelComm	KaChing	page 86
Paul Davies	The Last Three Minutes	page 29
David J. Schwartz	The Magic of Thinking Big	page 79

Michael D. Coe	*The Maya*	page	84
Dan Schawbel	*Me 2.0*	page	15
Robert Spector	*The Mom & Pop Store*	page	150
Marlo Morgan	*Mutant Message Down Under*	page	110
Pam Lassiter	*The New Job Security, Revised*	page	146
Phil Simon	*The Next Wave of Technologies*	page	71
Christopher Hitchens	*No One Left To Lie To*	page	122
Mao Tse-tung	*On Guerrilla Warfare*	page	57
F. Gonzalez-Crussi	*On Seeing*	page	106
P.J. O'Rourke	*Peace Kills*	page	3
Seth Godin	*Permission Marketing*	page	73
Larry D. Rosen, Ph.D.	*Rewired*	page	90
Jason Fried, David Heinemeier Hansson, Mike Rohde	*Rework*	page	101
William T. Vollmann	*Riding Toward Everywhere*	page	75
James Redfield	*The Secret of Shambhala*	page	118
James M. Robinson	*The Secrets of Judas*	page	148

Snake and Other Poems
D.H. Lawrence   page 126

Social Media 101
Chris Brogan   page 38

Social Media Metrics
Jim Sterne   page 55

Songs of Milarepa
Milarepa   page 24

Strange Maine
Michelle Souliere   page 144

SuperFreakonomics
Steven D. Levitt, Stephen J. Dubner   page 22

Traveler's Guide to The Ancient World –
Ancient Egypt: Thebes and the Nile Valley in the Year 1200 BCE
Charlotte Booth   page 66

Traveler's Guide to The Ancient World –
Ancient Greece: Athens and its Environs in the Year 415 BCE
Eric Chaline   page 66

Traveler's Guide to The Ancient World –
The Roman Empire: Rome and its Environs in the Year 300 CE
Dr. Ray Laurence   page 66

Tribes
Seth Godin   page 154

Trust Agents
Chris Brogan, Julien Smith   page 26

The Twitter Job Search Guide:
Susan Britton Whitcomb, Chandlee Bryan, Deb Dib   page 124

Twitterville
Shel Israel   page 77

The Union of Their Dreams
Miriam Pawel   page   9

UnMarketing
Scott Stratten   page 131

Use Your Head to Get Your Foot in the Door
Harvey Mackay   page   51

Utopia
Sir Thomas More   page   44

Viral Loop
Adam L. *Penenberg*   page   40

Vitamin Q
Roddy Lumsden   page   133

Well Connected
Gordon S. Curtis   page   112

What Bothers Me Most about Christianity
Ed Gungor   page   98

What Your Body Says
Sharon Sayler   page   94

Whispers
Ronald K. Siegel   page   120

Who Moved My Mouse?
Dena Harris   page   142

A World Without Islam
Graham E. Fuller   page   137

The Writer's Voice
A. Alvarez   page   46

www.ingramcontent.com/pod-product-compliance
Lightning Source LLC
Chambersburg PA
CBHW060519100426
42743CB00009B/1375